HOWARD'S LONG MARCH

The Strategic Depiction of China
in Howard Government Policy,
1996–2006

HOWARD'S LONG MARCH

The Strategic Depiction of China
in Howard Government Policy,
1996–2006

ROY CAMPBELL MCDOWALL

ANU
THE AUSTRALIAN NATIONAL UNIVERSITY

E PRESS

ANU

E PRESS

Published by ANU E Press
The Australian National University
Canberra ACT 0200, Australia
Email: anuepress@anu.edu.au
This title is also available online at: http://epress.anu.edu.au/howard_march_citation.html

National Library of Australia
Cataloguing-in-Publication entry

Author: Campbell McDowall, Roy.

Title: Howard's long march : the strategic depiction of China in
                Howard government policy 1996-2006 / Roy Campbell McDowall.

ISBN: 9781921536441 (pbk.)   9781921536458 (pdf.)

Notes: Includes index.
                Bibliography.

Subjects: Australia--Politics and government--1996-
                Australia--Foreign economic relations--China.
                China--Foreign economic relations--Australia.
                Australia--Foreign relations--China
                China--Foreign relations--Australia.
                 Australia--Foreign relations--United States.
                United States--Foreign relations--Australia
                United States--Foreign relations--China.
                China--Foreign relations--United States.

Dewey Number: 337.94051

The *Canberra Papers on Strategy and Defence* series is a collection of publications arising
principally from research undertaken at the SDSC. Canberra Papers have been peer reviewed
since 2006. All Canberra Papers are available for sale: visit the SDSC website at <http://rspas.
anu.edu.au/sdsc/canberra_papers.php> for abstracts and prices. Electronic copies (in pdf
format) of most SDSC Working Papers published since 2002 may be downloaded for free from
the SDSC website at <http://rspas.anu.edu.au/sdsc/working_papers.php>. The entire Working
Papers series is also available on a 'print on demand' basis.

Cover design by ANU E Press

Contents

Abstract

Because Australia is facing the prospect of its largest trade partner (China) becoming a strategic adversary of Australia's major ally (United States), how Australia depicts China's rise has become a salient foreign policy issue. This investigation argues that the former Howard Government's predominant *depiction* of China was positive, but that its predominant *perception* of China was one of mistrust and unease. According to this investigation, positive depictions of China are motivated by insecurity rather than genuine strategic reorientation towards China. Three distinct periods can be discerned in the mood of Australia-China relations, and corresponding depictions, between 1996 and 2006. Period One (1996) was characterised by positive *policy* depictions, and negative *crisis* depictions. Period Two (1997–2002) was characterised by predominantly positive depictions, with occasionally cautious depictions. Period Three (2003–2006) observed depictions of strategic alignment, with, yet again, several cautious depictions. This paper argues that the Howard Government positively depicted China as part of a regional hedging strategy. Positive depictions serve three objectives. First, they compel the United States to work harder at strengthening its security alliances in the region. Second, they allay Chinese fears of containment and convince China that its 'peaceful development' diplomacy is allowing it to successfully engage and integrate into the region. Third, in the case of the Howard Government, they shut down an avenue of domestic criticism towards its foreign policy. Hedging reveals that the Howard Government was a complex actor, in contrast to descriptions of it as a 'response agent' conducting a 'hope based formula' of engagement with China.

About the Author

Roy Campbell McDowall was born in New Plymouth, New Zealand. After completing his BA(Hons) at the University of Auckland, he moved to Canberra in 2006.

In June 2007 he successfully completed a Master of Arts (Strategic Studies) in the Graduate Studies in Strategy and Defence program at The Australian National University.

In 2009 he is commencing a PhD at The Australian National University, examining Indonesia in Australia's defence planning under the supervision of the Strategic and Defence Studies Centre.

Acknowledgements

Special thanks are extended to Dr Brendan Taylor, supervisor and friend, for his tireless assistance. His support and advice have been invaluable. Academic support was also contributed by Professor Hugh White, Dr Robert Ayson and Dr Ron Huisken, to whom I extend many thanks. The enduring support of my parents, Jim and Joce McDowall, and family, has been irreplaceable. Warm regards is due to the Strategic and Defence Studies Centre and the New Zealand Vice-Chancellors Committee for their generous financial support, which made this endeavour a pleasure rather than a pain. Joyous thanks are extended to my fellow students who endured with me the highs and lows of 'life in the lab'. My warmest regards to Mrs Sarah Flint, Ms Ping Yu, Miss Meredith Thatcher and Ms Altaire Harris for their ever present support. Special mention is made to Erlina Widyaningsih, whose constant support has been exceptional.

Introduction

With the electoral defeat of the Howard Government, it is timely to assess the Howard Government's strategic depiction of China. The question of how to strategically depict China and its threat potential without arousing Chinese hostility or suspicion has been a taxing issue for successive Australian governments, including the Howard Government. During the past 30 years, as China's place in the Australian economy has steadily grown, the issue of how to depict China has increased in importance and complexity. Today, China's new status as Australia's largest trade partner secures its importance in Australian strategic policy alongside the United States, Japan and Indonesia.[1] But, at the same time, growing tension in Australia's foreign policy between economic interest (China) and security interest (the United States) is observable. Australia is facing the prospect of its largest trading partner (China) becoming a strategic adversary of Australia's major ally (the United States).[2] How Australia balances its economic and security interests is a demanding foreign policy conundrum. During a time of watchful strategic competition in US-China relations, Australia's strategic depiction of China remains a key indicator of Australia's response to the rise of China and the shifting distribution of power in the Asia-Pacific region. Therefore, as the Rudd Government begins to construct its own strategic depictions of China, it is important to appreciate the strengths and weaknesses of the Howard Government's approach towards China and to identify what aspects require retention, adjustment or rejection.

Ever since its early days in office, the Howard Government's strategic depiction of China was a source of debate and intrigue. In March 1996, the then Foreign Minister Alexander Downer declared unequivocal support for two US carrier groups deployed to the Taiwan Strait.[3] Over the course of time, other captivating statements were made. In May 2000 Prime Minister John Howard singled out high-technology Australian Defence Force assets for a Taiwan contingency.[4] The Department of Foreign Affairs and Trade White Paper of 2003, *Advancing the National Interest: Australia's Foreign and Trade Policy White Paper*, described Australia's relationship with China as a 'strategic economic partnership', and in August 2004 Downer declared the existence of a 'strategic relationship' between Australia and China.[5] Obviously the Howard Government's strategic depiction of China evolved remarkably over this timeframe. Understanding what these depictions, and others, meant in the context of Australia-China relations, Australia-US relations, Australia-US-China relations, and Australia's broader strategic orientation in the Asia-Pacific are a salient foreign policy issue for Australia. Because of China's growing potential to compete strategically with the United States, the possibility of US-China conflict over Taiwan, and the centrality of China to Australia's economic interests, it is key for Australia to do whatever it can to reduce the probability of conflict. Although the degree of influence Australia possesses in this regard is contestable, the considerable diplomatic effort by China to promote its 'peaceful development' suggests that how the Asia-Pacific region responds is important to Beijing, and Washington.[6] How Australia depicts China can certainly influence the latter's strategic perceptions and its corresponding strategic behaviour, and US attitudes towards China's rise.[7] Examining Australia's strategic depiction of China between 1996 and 2006 therefore provides key insights into the possible future trajectory of Australia's foreign policy and a vital case study into the broader regional issue of how countries in the Asia-Pacific are responding to the rise of China.

This investigation complements and builds upon research conducted by Lachlan Strahan, Mohan Malik, Zhang Jian, Michael Wesley and Paul Kelly. Strahan has provided a comprehensive investigation of Australia's view of China from the 1930s to the 1990s and, with the passage of time, his analysis can now be updated.[8] Malik and Zhang have produced chronological surveys of Australia-China relations in the period 1996–2005.[9] Malik recognises two phases in the 1996–2000 period: an initial phase of acrimony and hostility during 1996, followed by a period of reconciliation from 1997 to 2000. Malik notes that, while the relationship is observing commercial convergence, broader regional developments indicate strategic divergence is occurring between the two countries. He believes that if China assumes a more aggressive regional posture, especially towards Taiwan, the ANZUS alliance will quickly assume a containment posture. Zhang regards the warmth of relations between Australia and China during the period 2001–2005 as a by-product of healthy US-China relations. He believes the 'war on terror' has provided a strategic distraction to the rise of China, and that Australia-China relations will deteriorate once the United States resets its vision towards China. Malik's and Zhang's valuable contributions have mapped the general events occurring within the relationship, and provide a firm foundation from which to conduct in-depth analysis upon the strategic dimension of the relationship.

Adopting slightly different research focuses, Wesley has produced a broader thematic analysis of Howard Government diplomacy in Asia, and Kelly a character analysis of former Prime Minister John Howard. Wesley's investigation concludes that although the Howard Government successfully conducted a period of deepened engagement with China, its 'hope based formula' presuming continuing stability in US-China relations was an inadequate policy to guide one of Australia's most demanding foreign policy challenges.[10] Wesley's investigation reveals that deeper consideration is required concerning the nature of the Howard Government's engagement policy with China, which at face value appeared simplistic. Kelly's analysis of the effect of the executive branch on Australian foreign policy is a compelling read. One of Kelly's key portrayals of Howard is as a 'response agent', a person who reacted to, rather than engineered, his political surrounds. Like Wesley's 'hope based formula', Kelly's observation of Howard (and subsequently the Howard Government) as a 'response agent' provides a provocative theory of the Howard Government as an opportunistic and even naïve political actor. This demands deeper analysis.

By examining the Howard Government's strategic depiction of China during the decade in question, this investigation seeks to answer a series of pivotal questions left unanswered by the research of Strahan, Malik, Zhang, Wesley and Kelly. These questions include whether a coherent policy vision was implemented or whether an ad hoc process of policy evolution was instead at work. (Indeed, a synthesis of the two may be possible: a coherent, yet evolutionary policy formulating process may have been in operation). The answers to these questions will clarify the nature of Australia's relationship with China, and assist in answering larger questions regarding the emergence, evolution and exact nature of Australia's strategic interaction with China. Specifically, the answers will reveal whether Kelly's description of Howard as a 'response agent' is accurate and applicable to the Howard Government, and whether Wesley's 'hope based formula' accurately describes Howard Government policy towards China. In turn, answering these larger questions will provide valuable insight into the future trajectory of the relationship, and the role of depictions in international relations.

In his seminal work *The Logic of Images in International Relations*, Robert Jervis describes his investigation of strategic depictions as providing 'the foundation for a theory of deception in international relations'.[11] According to Jervis, strategic depictions are 'the way states can affect the images others have of them and thereby exercise influence without paying the high cost of altering their own major policies'.[12] Depictions often provide essential images of how a government *wants to be viewed*, rather than an accurate portrayal of what a government's perceptions actually are. Jervis divided strategic depictions into two main categories: signals and indices. Signals are 'a state's direct statements of intention', whether they are private (diplomacy) or public (policy) statements.[13] They consist of varied and diverse methods of communication, such as policy statements, diplomatic notes, military manoeuvres, and extending or breaking diplomatic relations. In contrast, indices have a more subjective value, imparted by the strategic analyst. In essence, indices are actions and statements that are judged by the strategic analyst to be 'too important to be used for deception' because the state is either unaware its behaviour is being observed, or the state is unable to control its behaviour in a deceptive manner, usually because of the high profile status of the data.[14]

Evidently, strategic depictions are complex phenomena. They are the substance of strategic communication, granting insight into a state's strategic perspective, and how a state desires its strategic outlook to be perceived by other states. They provide windows into the strategic interests of a government and its polity. The Howard Government's strategic depiction of China was a message to China, the United States and the entire Asia-Pacific region, conveying how Australia strategically viewed China from 1996 until 2006, and how it desired its strategic outlook to be perceived by other states.[15] It is a complex dialogue, to more than one audience, and it is an evolving rather than a static dialogue. Strategic depictions are the 'language' of strategy, imparting knowledge of broader strategic trends.[16] Depictions can also reveal the influence of contextual circumstances, as a barometer of how relations between two states are faring. Furthermore, strategic depictions are not mere commentaries on strategic phenomena; they possess considerable strategic weight in the considerations of grand strategy. Consequently, in the field of Australian strategic studies the former Howard Government's strategic depiction of China is a seminal topic. How it viewed China had a genuine impact on Australia's strategic environs today. Thus Australia's depictions of China are important not only for providing clear transparent communication of Australia's perspective on the rise of China, but also for trying to influence the strategic behaviour of China and other regional actors, particularly the United States, Japan and country members of the Association of Southeast Asian Nations.

This investigation draws upon a number of primary sources of strategic depictions, including policy statements, as well as government speeches and media releases. It is divided into three chapters. Research results indicate three discernible changes in the mood and rhetoric of Howard Government depictions of China and Australia-China relations between 1996 and 2006. These are Period One (March 1996 to December 1996), Period Two (January 1997 to December 2002) and Period Three (January 2003 to December 2006). Period One was characterised by frequent diplomatic disputes between Australia and China, and may be regarded as a period of relationship deterioration. While Howard Government *policy* depictions of China remained very positive, the mood of the relationship was extremely poor. January 1997 to December 2002 is distinguishable from the other periods as a time of relatively stable relations between the two countries, bolstered by a booming trade relationship. Although diplomatic disputes did arise frequently, these were successfully navigated around as economic interests took firm precedence. It can be characterised as a period of relationship restoration and intensification. The third period, January 2003 to December 2006, can be characterised as a period of relationship ambiguity, or 'friendly unease'. The key phrase in the 2003 White Paper, 'strategic economic relationship', opened new possibilities for interpreting the relationship in contrast to the distinctly economic driven vision of the previous six years.[17] While the economic relationship remained vibrant and central to the relationship, new strategic dimensions were becoming apparent in Howard Government rhetoric.

Having examined these three periods this investigation will submit concluding remarks. In brief, an overarching theme of this investigation is the tension between economic opportunity and strategic anxiety caused by China's rise. The investigation observes that, although the Howard Government's dominant *depiction* of China was positive, a persistent but subtle theme of strategic unease was discernible. This indicates that a resilient and persistent strategic *perception* of doubt and unease was evident within the Howard Government in relation to China's rise. Consequently, across the Howard years a coherent, deliberate policy of positive depictions was implemented. It can be argued that a steady and coherent evolution occurred in the government's depiction of the Australia-China relationship, from an economic relationship (1996), to an economic relationship with strategic significance (1997), to a strategic economic relationship (2003) and, finally, to an explicit strategic relationship (2004). This evolution, of predominantly positive depictions and occasionally cautious depictions, arguably served a Howard Government hedging strategy in the region. This hedging strategy was aimed in particular at the dual goals of a strong ANZUS alliance and US presence in the region, and the peaceful development and accommodation of China into the Asia-Pacific security architecture. The Howard Government's hedging behaviour reflected the actions of the United States and China in the Asia-Pacific region, who lead the region in their hedging activities. According to Evan S. Medeiros,

> the United States and China are pursuing policies that, on one hand, stress engagement and integration mechanisms and, on the other, emphasize realist style balancing in the form of external security cooperation with Asian states and national military modernization programs.[18]

In Australia's case, hedging involved building a strong ANZUS alliance and US-led regional security structure, while engaging and accommodating China at the same time. Recent events, such as the discussion of a trilateral missile defence system between the United States, Australia and Japan, provide strong supporting evidence for the case that Australia was hedging, rather than being drawn into a Chinese sphere of influence.[19] By hedging, Australia was able to conduct a low-risk engagement program with China while bolstering its regional security partnerships. This policy served as an insurance guarantee: regardless of the future security environment—whether it be the ideal peaceful development and integration of China into the Asia-Pacific security architecture, or a less favourable, adversarial US-China balance of power system—Australian security would be ensured. Finally, this investigation briefly examines the utility of the

Howard Government's hedging strategy, and whether other viable policy alternatives were available to it.

ENDNOTES

[1] Trade in the financial year to March 2007 with China grossed A$52.7 billion, surpassing Australia's trade with Japan of A$50.6 billion. See David Uren, 'China emerges as our biggest trade partner, *Australian*, 5 May 2007, available at <http://www.theaustralian.news.com.au/printpage/0,5942,21674786,00.html>, accessed 8 May 2007.

[2] Hugh White, 'The limits to optimism: Australia and the rise of China', *Australian Journal of International Affairs*, vol. 59, no. 4, December 2005, p. 478.

[3] Don Greenlees and Richard McGregor, 'Downer warns China over war games', *Australian*, 13 March 1996, p. 8.

[4] Prime Minister John Howard, 'Interview with Steve Liebmann', 5 May 2000, available at <http://www.pm.gov.au/media/interview/2000/today0505.cfm>, accessed 1 April 2007.

[5] Department of Foreign Affairs and Trade, *Advancing the National Interest: Australia's Foreign and Trade Policy White Paper*, Commonwealth of Australia, Canberra, 2003, p. xv; and Foreign Minister Alexander Downer, 'Media Conference', Beijing, 17 August 2004, available at <http://www.foreignminister.gov.au/transcripts/2004/040817_ds_beijing.html>, accessed 2 April 2007.

[6] 'Peaceful development' has become the preferred phrase within Chinese foreign policy to describe China's rise, rather than the more disputable 'peaceful rise' term. See *People's Daily Online* at <http://english.people.com.cn/zhuanti/Zhuanti_458.html>, accessed 28 November 2008.

[7] 'China's Military Modernization and Cross-Strait Balance', hearing before the US-China Economic and Security Review Commission, One Hundred Ninth Congress, First Session, 15 September 2005, p. 232.

[8] Lachlan Strahan, *Australia's China: Changing perceptions from the 1930s to the 1990s*, Cambridge University Press, Cambridge, 1996, p. 289.

[9] Mohan Malik, 'Australia and China: Divergence and Convergence of Interests', in James Cotton and John Ravenhill (eds), *Australia in World Affairs 1996-2000*, Oxford University Press, Oxford, 2001, pp. 109–129; and Zhang Jian, 'Australia and China: Towards a Strategic partnership?', in James Cotton and John Ravenhill (eds), *Australia in World Affairs 2001-2005*, Oxford University Press, Oxford, 2001, pp. 89–111.

[10] Michael Wesley, *The Howard Paradox: Australian Diplomacy in Asia 1996-2006*, ABC Books, Sydney, 2007, p. 218.

[11] Robert Jervis, *The Logic of Images in International Relations*, Princeton University Press, Princeton, 1970, p. 10.

[12] Jervis, *The Logic of Images in International Relations*, p. 3.

[13] Jervis, *The Logic of Images in International Relations*, p. 20.

[14] Jervis, *The Logic of Images in International Relations*, p. 28.

[15] As one commentator has noted, policy has four different audiences—the individual policy department that produced the statement, the government in general, the domestic audience, and the international audience. Often these audiences are ranked accordingly. Interview with former Howard Government employee.

[16] Jervis, *The Logic of Images in International Relations*, p. 21.

[17] Department of Foreign Affairs and Trade, *Advancing the National Interest*, p. 79.

[18] Evan S. Medeiros, 'Strategic Hedging and the Future of Asia-Pacific Stability', *The Washington Quarterly*, vol. 29, no. 1 (Winter 2005–06), pp. 145–67 at p. 145.

[19] Alexander Downer, 'Joint press conference with US Secretary of State Condoleezza Rice', Ronald Reagan Library, Simi Valley, California, 24 May 2007, available at <http://www.foreignminister.gov.au/transcripts/2007/070524_jpc_rice.html>, accessed 25 May 2007.

Chapter 1

Setting the Vision amongst a Sea of Troubles: March–December 1996

Describing the Howard Government's strategic depiction of China in 1996 is a complicated task because of two distinctly different factors at work within the Australia-China relationship, operating relatively independently of one another. On the one hand, the government was subject to a series of diplomatic disputes with China that saw the relationship sour to its lowest point in its 24-year history.[1] This compelled the government to depict China as a strategic problem. On the other hand, the government frequently cited its intent to engage and expand its ties with Asia more generally, and with China in particular. Thus China was also depicted as an economic opportunity. And, behind the scenes, trade relations between the two countries were largely unaffected by the disputes.[2] In brief, 1996 was characterised by positive *policy* depictions, and negative *crisis* depictions. Therefore, a simple chronological analysis of the year does not capture the essence of the period; a juxtaposition of two competing and overlapping factors—policy and environment. To provide a chronological analysis of 1996 only blurs the distinct message that each factor produced. Consequently, an analysis that does not recognise the relatively independent nature of these forces can only observe contradiction rather than coherence in the Howard Government's strategic depiction of China throughout 1996. Accordingly, a separate analysis of the incoming government's foreign policy vision for engagement with Asia and China is provided, followed by a review of the disputes and crises of 1996 and how these affected the government's depiction of China. Finally an assessment and comparison of these two distinct depictions—opportunity (policy) and problem (environment)—will be made.

When the Howard Government entered office on 11 March 1996 the Australian public remained uncertain in regards to how the new administration would approach relations with Asian countries such as China. During the 1996 election campaign the incumbent Labor Government led by Prime Minister Paul Keating had accused John Howard of abandoning Asia.[3] Keating attacked Howard, claiming 'the leadership of South-East Asia does not believe that the Coalition is serious about the relationship'.[4] Consequently, the government began its first term determined to denounce its critics' allegations that Asian governments would reject it. After only one month in office, the Foreign Minister, Alexander Downer, declared in his first major policy speech that 'closer engagement with Asia is the Australian Government's *highest foreign policy priority*.[5] This early declaration of intent negates the common perception that the Howard Government was adhering to an ANZUS dominated foreign policy when it entered office. Instead, Downer conveyed opportunism combined with a heightened sense of purpose and vision. He claimed 'the next 50 years will therefore depend on the decisions made over the next five'.[6] Specifically regarding China, Downer stated that 'Australia's relationship with China [would] remain a central feature of Australian foreign policy' and that 'the Australian government [would] maintain [its] one-China policy'.[7] Hence it can be observed that, early into its administration, the Howard Government's policy concerning China continued many of the positions held by the previous Labor Government. The status quo 'one-China' policy remained entrenched and Australia's relationship with China was classified under the unremarkable phrase 'central feature'.[8]

Although Downer's maiden declaratory speech of Howard Government foreign policy contained emotive references to the future, it remained unclear what the government was actually offering concerning foreign policy innovation towards Asia and China. However, there were some indications that subtle changes in Australian foreign policy were about to be implemented. A characteristic of the government's diplomacy would be bilateral rather than multilateral diplomatic initiatives. Downer declared that 'the third way the government [would] promote engagement in Asia is by strengthening the focus on bilateral relations'.[9] The motivation for this heightened bilateral engagement with the Asia-Pacific came from the growth of regional economies and economic interests, which enabled a corresponding development of military power. Downer said:

> Over the longer term economic development will lead to shifts in relative power and is likely to have an impact on the pattern of regional security relations. Economic development is already giving Asia-Pacific governments the means to acquire greater defensive capacities than in the past. These factors have the potential, if appropriate steps are not taken, to destabilise existing security patterns, heighten tensions and reduce security throughout the region.[10]

Thus the potential for escalating strategic competition in the region was clearly identified by the Howard Government. China's rise represented both an economic opportunity and a strategic challenge. Therefore, an inherent tension within Howard Government policy was the relationship between promoting economic prosperity and promoting strategic stability. As regional economies developed so would defence capabilities. How to engineer a prosperous and peaceful region rather than a prosperous and potent region presented a long-term challenge for the Howard Government. Indeed, the government claimed that it would adopt a 'long view' towards security and stability in the Asia-Pacific, and would be 'hard headed about security'.[11]

Although the government abstained from making explicit reference to China in these security statements, it was clear that the locus of regional instability was yoked to the economic rise of China and its corresponding power. Downer extrapolated:

> In the short to medium term, the primary objective of Australia's regional security policy will be to discourage the emergence of strategic confrontation in the Asia Pacific region. To this end, the Australian Government will be working to help bring regional countries closer to each other, by contributing to the building of constructive security arrangements in the region. Strengthening the web of Australia's bilateral security links will make a positive contribution to discouraging regional strategic competition.[12]

Coming only 30 days after the Taiwan Strait crisis, it was clear to whom the reference 'strategic confrontation' was being made.[13] However, Downer's rhetoric was delicate enough to discuss China's destabilising strategic effect in the region via the defence policies of Japan, South Korea and the United States. In September he explained to a New York audience:

> There is, I think, widespread support for continuing United States strategic engagement in the Asia-Pacific which underpins the region's stability and security. The United States has a vital role in helping to stabilise regional security. Your country's presence strengthens regional countries' confidence in their security—in effect helping to minimise tensions and maintain balance. This is most obvious in North East Asia where, for example, Japan and South Korea have not only refrained from acquiring nuclear weapons but have also undertaken legal obligations never to acquire them.[14]

Remembering that this statement was made only three months after the Chinese nuclear test (8 June 1996), the veiled reference to Chinese actions was unmistakable. While Japan and South Korea had maintained anti-proliferation stances, China's nuclear actions were destabilising.

Regardless of the issue of Chinese proliferation of Weapons of Mass Destruction, the Howard Government kept an optimistic outlook towards the creation of a stable regional order. China posed a strategic challenge, but the Howard Government believed bilateral engagement supplemented by a strong US presence in the region would soften the impact of China's rise. Downer maintained that, in the region's 'fluid, complex and uncertain' state, a 'window of opportunity' existed to invest heavily in a stable and secure future.[15] In his words 'Australia and its neighbours must make the most of the present relatively benign security environment to set in place stable and enduring security arrangements'.[16] This was an insightful glance into Australia's view of the region, and China. Despite the difficulties being experienced in Australia-China relations, the government regarded the security environment as reasonably 'benign'—a term traditionally employed sparingly in describing Australia's regional security environment. But the question of how to approach China remained problematic. In July, Downer announced that, 'strategically, China, and our long-term relationship with it, is of vital importance in Australia's foreign policy'.[17] Thus, between March and July 1996, the Howard Government continued to emphasise the importance of China as a 'central feature' in Australian foreign policy and the Australia-China relationship as an aspect of 'vital importance'.[18] This may have been an early characteristic of the government's 'practical bilateralism' coming into effect.[19] Even with the unfriendly mood of Australia-China diplomatic relations at the time, the government was persisting with its new emphasis upon bilateral engagement with China and the region.

To summarise, within a nine month period the Howard Government had clearly articulated its interest in engaging Asia, including China, as its highest foreign policy priority. This was to be conducted under the guise of 'practical bilateralism'.[20] In addition, there were tentative signs that Australia was beginning to consider its relations with China in strategic terms, describing the Australia-China relationship as a 'vital' strategic interest.[21] And, somewhat extraordinarily, the government regarded the regional security environment as 'relatively benign', despite the storm surrounding Australia-China relations.[22] Indeed, 1996 was not memorable for the foreign policy vision being declared by the Howard Government. Instead, the year was marked by a series of diplomatic crises between Australia and China.

When the Howard Government took office on 11 March 1996 it entered a regional political maelstrom. A serious diplomatic crisis between China and Taiwan had escalated with the deployment of two US aircraft carrier groups to the region. The crisis appeared reminiscent of a 'perfect storm': a novice Australian Government thrown unwittingly into one of the region's most serious strategic crisis since the Tiananmen Square uprising between April and June 1989. In an unprecedented step, Downer declared unequivocal support for the US forces deployed in the region, stating:

> I think what we have seen in the last few days is a very clear demonstration by the United States that it is interested in maintaining its involvement in the security of the region and we obviously welcome that.[23]

Downer's definitive declaration of support for the United States appeared to be the catalyst for arguably the most abysmal year in the history of

Australia-China relations. A sense of impending doom hung over the Australia-China relationship as the Howard Government appeared to confirm its critics' worst predictions.[24] Downer's unambiguous support for US involvement in the crisis was not recanted. The Taiwan Strait crisis was quickly followed in April by the discarding of the Development Import Finance Facility, invoking further Chinese protests. The Facility was a concessionary finance scheme for developing countries. China and a number of affected countries lodged official complaints with the Howard Government.[25]

In July 1996 the inaugural Asia-Pacific Cities Summit was held in Brisbane. Unfortunately, to the disdain of the Howard Government, the attendance of the Mayor of Taipei City, Chen Shui-ban (a leading pro-independence advocate within Taiwan's Democratic Progressive Party), was protested by the Chinese Government. A storm erupted concerning speculation that the Howard Government would bar the entry of Chen. However, such an outcome did not eventuate, and the Mayors of Beijing and Shenzhen declined to attend in protest.[26]

The inaugural Australia–United States Ministerial Consultations were held in Sydney from 25–27 July 1996 and proved to be a landmark event. Gathering the respective Defence and Foreign Ministers of Australia and the United States, the meeting climaxed with the 'Sydney Declaration'—a joint security declaration citing the ANZUS alliance's relevance and purpose heading into the twenty-first century. It reinforced the Howard Government's image as a stalwart of US interests in the region, describing the United States and Australia as 'natural allies'.[27] Recognising the security difficulties of the Asia-Pacific region, the Sydney statement declared:

> The ANZUS Treaty has long given shape and expression to the advancement of our common interests. During these challenging times in the strategic development of the region, both countries take this opportunity to reaffirm their mutual commitment to the obligations flowing from the Treaty.[28]

The Sydney Declaration went on to declare the goals of developing democracy, economic prosperity and strategic stability within the Asia-Pacific region. This vision was to be conducted within a bilateral framework strategy, with the specific objectives of preventing conflict, the proliferation of Weapons of Mass Destruction, and arms build-ups.[29] Although the Sydney Declaration did not refer explicitly to China, it was poorly received by Beijing. Following a similar US-Japan joint security statement in April 1996, the Sydney Declaration appears to have encouraged China to allege that a new US containment strategy was being forged in the region, in which Australia and Japan were two claws of a US crab.[30]

Chinese protests notwithstanding, the context in which AUSMIN occurred needs to be understood. Only two months prior to AUSMIN, China had conducted a nuclear test on 8 June 1996. Caught in the middle of Australia's diplomatic drive in the United Nations to establish a Comprehensive Test Ban Treaty, the Chinese nuclear test represented another Chinese snub to Australian diplomatic efforts. Having taken a lead role in advocating the Treaty, the Howard Government was cornered by its own policy position and had no choice but to strongly condemn the Chinese test.[31]

At the same time new revelations were coming to light. To its embarrassment the Howard Government admitted to conducting secret negotiations with Taiwan to sell uranium.[32] After pushing for the creation of a Comprehensive Test Ban Treaty, Australia's negotiations with Taiwan appeared to contradict its anti-proliferation objectives. A Ministerial visit to Taiwan by Primary Industries Minister John Anderson in September (possibly in association with the uranium trade negotiations) was met with strong Chinese opposition.[33] On 26 September 1996, after much speculation, Prime Minister Howard met the spiritual leader of Tibet, the Dalai Lama.[34] Once again the Howard Government incurred strong protests from China.

The final controversy of 1996, the Pauline Hanson debacle, was arguably the most damaging event to the Howard Government's overseas image. Hanson's One Nation Party had come to public prominence after achieving modest electoral success and polarising public debate regarding immigration. Hanson, formerly a Liberal candidate, was ejected from Howard's Liberal Party after making controversial remarks concerning 'race-based welfare'.[35] However, One Nation's inflammatory remarks regarding immigration placed the Howard Government in a difficult position. In her maiden speech to Parliament, Hanson claimed Australia was 'in danger of being swamped by Asians'.[36] Having ridden on popular sentiment regarding Australian values, Howard was reluctant to damage his populist Australian image.[37] The Howard Government's inability to distance itself from Hanson was damaging in a year when Howard had repeatedly looked isolated from Asia and China. After several weeks of controversy, the government did distance itself from Hanson and One Nation, but the damage had already been done.

Into this dire situation an unlikely event occurred. In an unprecedented step, Chinese President Jiang Zemin held a personal meeting with Prime Minister Howard in Manila before the 1996 Asia-Pacific Economic Cooperation conference. The Howard/Jiang meeting stands as a sign-post of a terrible year; an unofficial crisis meeting was required to repair the damaged Australia-China relationship. After the meeting Howard commented:

> We both agreed that the relationship was a strong one and could be made stronger. I think we established on a personal basis a very good rapport.

I said that despite the fact that Australia and China had some very basic differences so far as our political systems were concerned, and [*sic*] our size; that we had a lot of mutual interest, and that we should focus on those, that I would take a commonsense, practical approach to the relationship. At the end of the meeting the President invited me to visit China and I accepted that invitation and we are both going to work towards a visit by me to China in the first half of next year.[38]

Thus Howard had in many respects retrieved a position that appeared unsalvageable. Acknowledging that relations 'could be made stronger', he secured an unlikely return visit to Beijing in 1997.[39] While political differences remained unavoidable, a 'commonsense' approach to the relationship was to be adopted.[40] However, much work remained to be done to cast the relationship in a positive light. Regarding Australia's strategic orientation towards China, and the particular sensitivity of whether Australia was pursuing a containment strategy against China, Howard said:

I made it clear that we weren't trying to contain China. I said that the close relationship between Australia and the United States was there because it was the mutual desire of Australia and the United States to have a close relationship. I told him that the relationship was not directed at anybody. It was a relationship having a momentum and a merit all of its own. He, to my thinking, accepted that. I believe that on both sides there was a desire to find points that reinforced the positives of the relationship.[41]

Clearly, the Howard Government's actions throughout the year had aroused Chinese suspicions, and earned Howard the dubious honour of a personal meeting with Jiang. Howard had secured China's attention, but for all the wrong reasons.

To conclude, the Howard/Jiang talks represent a decisive end to a tumultuous year. Despite repeated quarrels, the governments of Australia and China were able to walk into 1997 regarding each other with a degree of respect. The relationship had encountered a severe storm, yet had remained intact, albeit bruised and battered. Indeed, the Howard Government's first year in office appeared to confirm its pundits' derisions of it as a novice foreign policy practitioner. Downer's definitive declaration of support for the United States during the 1996 Taiwan Strait crisis commenced an abysmal year in the history of Australia-China relations. Events such as the Chinese nuclear test and the Sydney Declaration exposed the differences and distance between Australia and China. At first glance the incoming Howard Government's foreign policy appeared simplistic, advocating a reinvigorated ANZUS alliance alongside a populist leaning domestically driven agenda.[42] But these objectives tended to overshadow the clear enunciation of engagement with Asia that was being declared at the same time. Although the Howard Government's foreign policy performed poorly on the public stage, in reality a steady foundation for expanded engagement with Asia and with China was being laid. Therefore, the story of 1996 is a complex milieu of competing foreign policy objectives. While Paul Kelly's description of Howard as a 'response agent', subject to the winds of political fortune, is *generally* accurate, this investigation also observes a more complex individual and government at work.[43]

The Howard Government's strategic depiction of China in 1996 is Janus-faced, conveying both optimism and adversity. *Policy* depictions of China in 1996 showed a country that represented an economic opportunity and a strategic challenge, rather than a strategic problem as portrayed in the 1996 crisis environment. The government adopted many of the outgoing Keating Government's perspectives; Downer's 'fluid, complex and uncertain' region statement was a repeat of Labor Defence Minister Robert Ray's 1993 Strategic Review statement.[44] The government was forced to confront the regional instability that China's rise was causing, receiving a rude introduction to the sensitivities of Chinese foreign policy (Taiwan). Support for the Comprehensive Test Ban Treaty left Australia with no option but to make its views clear regarding Chinese actions; Downer declaring, 'I condemn the nuclear test conducted today by China'.[45]

The question of 1996 as Jiang Zemin and the world at large saw it, therefore, was whether Australia was becoming part of a US containment strategy towards China, having announced themselves 'natural allies'.[46] As this analysis has revealed, such statements indicate 1996 was the extreme rather than the rule for the future conduct of Australia-China relations. In contradiction to the negative image surrounding Australia-China relations, the Howard Government had declared 'strategically, China and our long term relationship with it, is of vital importance in Australia's foreign policy' and had also assessed the region's security environment to be 'relatively benign'.[47] Consequently, in the ensuing period (1997–2002), a remarkable transition would occur in Australia-China relations.

ENDNOTES

[1] The March 1996 Taiwan Strait crisis was quickly followed by the discarding of the Development Import Finance Facility in April, invoking further Chinese protests. A Taiwanese mayoral visit to Brisbane (July) soured relations, before the mood of Australia-China relations darkened further when China conducted a nuclear test (8 June), invoking Australia's condemnation. The inaugural Australia–United States Ministerial Consultations (26–27 July) provoked a Chinese accusation that Australia was part of a new US containment strategy. Negotiations for a uranium trade deal with Taiwan (August), a ministerial visit to Taiwan (September), Prime Minister John Howard's meeting with the Dalai Lama (September), and the Pauline Hanson debacle left the Howard Government's relations with China reeling. Details of AUSMIN can be found on the Department of Foreign Affairs and Trade website at <http://www.dfat.gov.au/geo/us/ausmin/index.html>, accessed 28 November 2008.

[2] Australia's exports to China for the financial year 1996–97 were A$3,584 million, marginally down on A$3,781 million in 1995–96. See Australian Bureau of Statistics, 'Australia's Export Markets', available

at <http://www.abs.gov.au/Ausstats/abs@.nsf/94713ad445ff1425ca25682000192af2/be75d8ff866cba97
ca256aaa007fe175!OpenDocument>, accessed 28 November 2008.

[3] Michael Wesley, *The Howard Paradox: Australian Diplomacy in Asia from 1996-2006*, ABC Books, Sydney, 2007, p. 8.

[4] Michael Dwyer and Louise Dodson, 'PM questions Howard's pull in Asia region', *Australian Financial Review*, 2 February 1996, p. 13.

[5] Alexander Downer, 'Australia and Asia: Taking the Long View', 'Address to the Foreign Correspondents' Association', Sydney, 11 April 1996, available at <http://www.dfat.gov.au/media/speeches/foreign/1996/asia-long.html>, accessed 8 March 2007. [emphasis added]

[6] Downer, 'Australia and Asia: Taking the Long View'.

[7] Downer, 'Australia and Asia: Taking the Long View'.

[8] Downer, 'Australia and Asia: Taking the Long View'.

[9] Downer, 'Australia and Asia: Taking the Long View'.

[10] Alexander Downer, 'Security through Cooperation', address to the International Institute for Strategic Studies/Strategic and Defence Studies Centre Conference, 'The New Security Agenda in the Asia Pacific Region', Canberra, 2 May 1996, available at <http://www.dfat.gov.au/media/speeches/foreign/1996/regsec5.html>, accessed 3 April 2007.

[11] Downer, 'Security through Cooperation', address to the IISS/SDSC Conference.

[12] Downer, 'Security through Cooperation', address to the IISS/SDSC Conference.

[13] Downer, 'Security through Cooperation', address to the IISS/SDSC Conference.

[14] Alexander Downer, 'The Asia Pacific: gearing up for the twenty first century: address to the Asia Society', New York, 27 September 1996, available at <http://parlinfoweb.aph.gov.au/piweb/view_document.aspx?ID=12124&TABLE=PRESSREL>, accessed 6 April 2007.

[15] Alexander Downer, 'Regional Cooperation and Security', address to the Australian College of Defence and Strategic Studies, Canberra, 6 December 1996, available at <http://www.dfat.gov.au/media/speeches/foreign/1996/regional_coop_security.html>, accessed 2 April 2007.

[16] Downer, 'Security through Cooperation', address to the IISS/SDSC Conference.

[17] Alexander Downer, 'Address at a joint Asia House/Austcham luncheon', Hong Kong, 4 July 1996, available at <http://www.dfat.gov.au/media/speeches/foreign/1996/hongkong.html>, accessed 31 March 2007.

[18] Downer, 'Address at a joint Asia House/Austcham luncheon'.

[19] Downer, 'Address at a joint Asia House/Austcham luncheon'.

[20] Downer, 'Address at a joint Asia House/Austcham luncheon'.

[21] Downer, 'Address at a joint Asia House/Austcham luncheon'.

[22] Downer, 'Security through Cooperation', address to the IISS/SDSC Conference.

[23] Don Greenlees and Richard McGregor, 'Downer warns China over war games', *Australian*, 13 March 1996, p. 8.

[24] Then incumbent Prime Minister Paul Keating predicted that a Howard Government would be rejected by Asian leaders. See Wesley, *The Howard Paradox*, p. 8.

[25] Stephen Sherlock, Foreign Affairs, Defence and Trade Group, 'Australia's Relations with China: What's the Problem?', *Current Issues Brief 23*, 1996–97, available at <http://www.aph.gov.au/library/pubs/CIB/1996-97/97cib23.htm>, accessed 28 November 2008.

[26] Sherlock, 'Australia's Relations with China: What's the Problem?'

[27] Alexander Downer and Ian McLachlan, 'Australia-United States: a strategic partnership for the twenty-first century: Sydney Statement: joint security declaration', Sydney, 27 July 1996, available at <http://parlinfoweb.aph.gov.au/piweb/view_document.aspx?ID=3379&TABLE=PRESSREL>, accessed 6 April 2007.

[28] Downer and McLachlan, 'Australia-United States: a strategic partnership for the twenty-first century: Sydney Statement: joint security declaration'.

[29] Downer and McLachlan, 'Australia-United States: a strategic partnership for the twenty-first century: Sydney Statement: joint security declaration'.

[30] Sherlock, 'Australia's Relations with China: What's the Problem?'

[31] Alexander Downer, 'Media release', 8 June 1996, available at <http://www.dfat.gov.au/media/releases/foreign/1996/fa46.html>, accessed 16 March 2007.

[32] Alexander Downer, 'Media release' 16 August 1996, available at <http://www.dfat.gov.au/media/releases/foreign/1996/fa80.html>, accessed 5 April 2007.

[33] Sherlock, 'Australia's Relations with China: What's the Problem?'

[34] Sherlock, 'Australia's Relations with China: What's the Problem?'

[35] Emma Dawson, 'What the PM owes to Hansonism', *Age*, 8 September 2006, available at <http://www.theage.com.au/news/opinion/what-the-pm-owes-to-hansonism/2006/09/07/1157222261242.html>, accessed 28 November 2008.

[36] Wesley, *The Howard Paradox*, p. 9.

[37] Downer in his first major foreign policy speech said: 'Australia is neither Asian nor American nor European. We are Australian and relate to our neighbours as Australians'. See Downer, 'Australia and Asia: Taking the Long View'.

[38] John Howard, 'Media release', 24 November 1996, available at <http://parlinfoweb.aph.gov.au/piweb/view_document.aspx?ID=9420&TABLE=PRESSREL>, accessed 7 April 2007.

[39] Howard, 'Media release', 24 November 1996.

[40] Howard, 'Media release', 24 November 1996.

[41] Howard, 'Media release', 24 November 1996.

[42] Paul Kelly, *Howard's decade: An Australian Foreign Policy Reappraisal*, Lowy Institute Paper no. 15, Lowy Institute for International Policy, Sydney, 2006, p. 3.

[43] Kelly, *Howard's decade: An Australian Foreign Policy Reappraisal*, p. 10.

[44] Lachlan Strahan, *Australia's China: Changing perceptions from the 1930s to the 1990s*, Cambridge University Press, Cambridge, 1996, p. 317.

[45] Downer, 'Media release', 8 June 1996.

[46] Downer and McLachlan, 'Australia-United States: a strategic partnership for the twenty-first century: Sydney Statement: joint security declaration'.

[47] Downer, 'Address at a joint Asia House/Austcham luncheon'; and Downer, 'Security through Cooperation', address to the IISS/SDSC Conference.

Chapter 2

Relationship Restoration and Expansion: January 1997– December 2002

In contrast to 1996, the Howard Government's strategic depiction of China throughout the period 1997–2002 is relatively uncomplicated. The government continued to depict China as an economic opportunity and strategic challenge simultaneously, although depictions of China as a strategic challenge were sparse. While the period is substantial in duration, a degree of consistency and coherence can be observed across it. The Australia-China relationship throughout this period is characterised by restoration and expansion and can be differentiated from 1996 for the remarkably positive mood of Australia-China relations throughout the period. Sensitivities in the relationship did surface on a number of occasions, with particular reference to Taiwan, but the atmosphere of the relationship remained relatively stable in contrast to the sour demeanour of relations in 1996. Therefore, this chapter will conduct a straightforward chronological analysis of the Howard Government's strategic depiction of China, and will be interrupted intermittently by the various disputes that complicated the largely harmonious relations.

Having presided over one of the worst periods in Australia-China relations history in 1996, the Howard Government entered 1997 under considerable pressure. While the trade relationship remained relatively buoyant throughout 1996, diplomatic relations were tense. Following the talks held in November 1996 with Chinese President Jiang Zemin in Manila, Howard visited Beijing in March 1997. The Beijing talks built upon the successful dialogue in Manila, restoring a degree of confidence in the relationship. In fact these talks may have been some of the most significant discussions of the Howard years. Within months, other Howard Government Ministers were lauding the significance of Howard's visit to Beijing. Downer said that 'Prime Minister Howard—during his China visit in late March—spoke with equal enthusiasm of a new economic "strategic partnership" between Australia and China'.[1] The Minister for Trade, Tim Fischer, also referred to Howard's conceptualisation of a new 'economic strategic partnership' with China during the Beijing visit, and noted that 'China has made a number of strategic and significant investments in Australia'.[2] Evidently the Howard Government's early indications in 1996 of associating Australia's economic interests with its strategic interests were continuing in 1997. The government's employment of the phrase 'strategic partnership' concerning economic relations is of particular interest, bringing the domains of strategic and economic interest closer together. Yet the phrase 'strategic partnership', when placed in association with economic interests, is confusing. Such a phrase makes defining exactly where economic interest ends and strategic interest begins a difficult task. This was a problem that would persist throughout the Howard years.[3] Although the Australia-China relationship remained firmly placed within the domain of economic interest, such statements revealed that the strategic significance of the economic relationship was becoming increasingly visible.

By April 1997 a very positive transition in the mood of Australia-China relations had occurred. Downer celebrated the 'new economic partnership',[4] stating: 'I am convinced that the recent expansion in our two-way investment links is an unmistakable sign of a maturing economic relationship.'[5] The warming of Australia-China relations was not limited to economic relations. In the security domain, the Australian Government announced the creation of a new annual dialogue between Australia and China. Downer said:

> During my visit to China in August last year, I proposed—and China agreed—to expand our annual bilateral disarmament discussions to include discussion of regional security issues. And, during the Prime Minister's recent visit, agreement was reached on initiating a regular dialogue between our defence agencies.[6]

Hence, after 13 months in office the Howard Government had established a number of security links with China which at the time were unprecedented in the history of Australia-China relations.[7] What appears significant was that these new security ties were Australian initiatives. The government was reaching out to China rather than vice versa, bringing China into the ranks of Australia's dialogue partners.

Building upon these ground-breaking security initiatives, on 10 April 1997 the Howard Government made an important shift in its diplomatic relations with China. It implemented a new approach towards one of the persisting sensitivities in the relationship—human rights. Instead of supporting an annual UN General Assembly resolution condemning China's human rights abuses, the government initiated a bilateral human rights dialogue with China. Downer declared 'China has agreed in principle to Australia's proposal, put by the Prime Minister to Premier Li Peng last week during his visit to China, that we establish a formal and regular bilateral dialogue on human rights'.[8] This represented an important move in Australia-China relations, departing from the conventional modes of engagement and critique conducted by many other Western countries in relation to China. While differences remained, from now on Australia-China differences concerning human rights would be addressed in private negotiations rather than on the public floor of the UN General Assembly. Even so, 1997 was not without its sensitivities and the new dialogue method was soon to be put to the test. Of particular concern was the hand-over of Hong Kong back to China. However, the Howard Government conducted smooth negotiations in support of the change-over and expressed concern for the continuation of 'the rule of law, the free flow of information, labour and capital; and the rights and freedoms the people of Hong Kong currently enjoy'.[9]

Having successfully distanced itself from the UN human rights debate with China, the Howard Government was set to declare a new era in Australia-China relations. The launch of the first Department of Foreign Affairs and Trade (DFAT) White Paper, *In the National Interest*, in August 1997, reflected a new tone of cautious optimism that was being restored to the relationship with China. In synchronisation with the policy declarations of 1996, the 1997 DFAT White Paper again emphasised the importance of strengthening bilateral ties in the region.[10] *In the National Interest* recognised the centrality of China to prosperity and security in the region, and acknowledged its important strategic role:

> China's economic growth, with attendant confidence and enhanced influence, will be the most important strategic development of the next fifteen years. How China manages its economic growth and pursues its international objectives, and how other nations, particularly the United States and Japan, respond to China will be crucial issues over the period.[11]

Having declared engagement with Asia its 'highest foreign policy priority' in 1996, the Howard Government now announced that China's rise was 'the most significant strategic development of the next fifteen years'.[12] The attention dedicated to Japan, China and the United States showed that the great power relations of Northeast Asia were viewed as pivotal to Australia's ongoing interest in a stable Asia-Pacific region. The White Paper said 'the effectiveness of Japanese and US policy towards China, and China's handling of its relations with them, will be key determinants of the future stability of East Asia'.[13] A degree of consistency was apparent with prior Howard Government statements regarding the economic and strategic importance of China. The White Paper recognised the Australia-China relationship as one of Australia's 'key' relationships and a degree of modesty in expectations was apparent, the DFAT White Paper emphasising mutual respect as

> a realistic framework for the conduct of the relationship, and offering the best prospects to maximise shared economic interests, advance Australia's political and strategic interests, and manage differences in a sensible and practical way. The one-China policy will continue to be a fundamental element of the bilateral relationship.[14]

Once again economic interests were clearly separated from strategic interests. The one-China policy remained the norm and differences would be negotiated in a sensible fashion. To summarise, *In the National Interest* identified China's economic rise as the most important strategic phenomenon in the region. China represented an opportunity and challenge that had to be engaged in a 'realistic' manner.[15] Thus, it is clear that DFAT depicted China as representing more of an opportunity than a threat.

However, other perspectives concerning China's rise were discernible within the Howard Government's departments. Despite the restoration of positive diplomatic relations and a buoyant trade relationship, a more cautionary view of China's rising power was held by the Department of Defence. In December 1997 the government released the 1997 Strategic Review, *Australia's Strategic Policy*, which included revealing commentary regarding Australia's strategic perception and depiction of China. The Strategic Review noted that 'China is already the most important factor for change in the regional strategic environment'.[16] This was complementary to DFAT's identification of China's rise as 'the most significant strategic development' in the region.[17] Crucially, the Strategic Review also noticed the improvement of China's power projection capabilities, stating that:

> Sustained high economic growth, and commensurate increases in defence funding, combined with access to more modern technology, especially from parts of the former Soviet Union, have increased China's strategic capabilities. Its air and maritime forces, in particular, are being developed at a significant pace, albeit from a low base.[18]

Naturally the development of China's power projection capabilities was of particular interest to the Department of Defence, as Australia's own territorial integrity remains founded on secure defence of the 'sea-air gap' surrounding Australia.[19] Although *Australia's Strategic Policy* conceded that China's capabilities were being developed from a 'low base', it also observed that the rate of change was occurring at a 'significant pace'.[20] Clearly the government was uncomfortable with this strategic development. Although the Strategic Review attempted to allay fears, stating 'this expansion of China's military capabilities does not constitute a threat to Australia', it went on to acknowledge that 'it would not be in Australia's interests for China's growing power to result in a dimunition [*sic*] of US strategic influence, or to stimulate damaging strategic competition between China and other regional powers'.[21]

Evidently the government remained uncomfortable with the prospect of a strategic environment dominated by China. And to dismiss China as a threat, having just described China's rising power, almost seemed a contradiction. If China was not a threat, why was the Howard Government concerned about the maintenance of the US presence in the region? Hence it must be considered decisive that *Australia's Strategic Policy* found Australia's primary strategic interest to be a continued US presence in the region. Without it, the government believed strategic instability would ensue. This reinforced the cautionary tone sometimes apparent within *In the National Interest*, which also stated that:

> Within East Asia, US strategic engagement in the region is widely regarded as a crucial stabilising influence, and an indispensable condition for the continuing strategic stability on which the region's economic success is ultimately dependent. Without it, regional countries might seek to significantly expand their defence capability in a destabilising way.[22]

Therefore anxiety can be observed in the Howard Government's strategic depiction of China, both in diplomacy (DFAT) and in defence (the Department of Defence). This was despite the overwhelming emphasis upon economic opportunity in the DFAT White Paper. As a result, the task at hand for Australia and the region according to *Australia's Strategic Policy* was to

> convince Beijing that China's legitimate interests and growing influence can be accommodated within the current regional framework. China will need to work hard to reassure the rest of the region that its national objectives and the means it uses to achieve them will be consistent with the basic interests of its neighbours.[23]

Echoing the DFAT White Paper, the Defence Strategic Review considered Australia's relationship with China as sharing economic interests but not strategic interests.[24] The Strategic Review repeated the DFAT White Paper word for word, stating:

> China will remain one of Australia's key relationships, with our approach based on shared interests and mutual respect. These principles provide the basis for a realistic framework for the conduct of the relationship, and offer the best prospects to maximise shared economic interests, advance Australia's political and strategic interests, and manage differences in a sensible and practical way.[25]

Clearly a coordinated DFAT/Defence approach to China was being conducted by the Howard Government. Despite the different objectives of the organisations in question, the strategic depictions of China that the two organs were conveying were generally very similar. Certainly the 1997 Strategic Review, despite displaying a cautionary tone towards China's rise, did conclude on a conciliatory theme, similar to the DFAT White Paper, commenting that China has 'legitimate claims as an emerging major power'.[26] However, the Strategic Review also noted that 'Japan's strategic interests converge quite strongly with Australia's. We share with Japan an interest in continuing US engagement, the freedom of navigation in the region, and the avoidance of increased strategic rivalry between the United States and China'.[27]

Hence, the open introduction of Japan into Australia's public strategic calculus regarding China was an important development. This action arguably displays a degree of reticence in the theory of China's 'peaceful development', and provides an early indication of the government contemplating a hedging strategy.[28]

In summary, the DFAT White Paper and Defence Strategic Review of 1997 provide an accurate reflection of the Howard Government's strategic depictions of China throughout the period 1997–2002. Even as the Australia-China economic relationship soared from strength to strength, both of these documents reflected a mood of strategic caution within the Howard Government.

Indeed, the period 1997–2002 was not without its challenges. The Asian Financial Crisis of 1997–98 severely damaged a number of Asian economies, and disturbed business confidence within the Asia-Pacific region. Yet this turned out to be a diplomatic windfall for Australia and China. Both countries' economies managed to ride through the crisis relatively unscathed. This boosted increasing Australian business confidence in the strength of the Chinese economy and, with it, government praise. During the financial crisis, Downer said that China's decision not to revalue the renminbi was 'a very positive step towards stabilising the region's economy'.[29]

Other sensitivities included the North Atlantic Treaty Organization bombing of the Chinese Embassy in Belgrade on 9 May 1999. This induced a prompt expression of regret and sympathy from the Howard Government.[30] Another issue centred on the release of businessman James Peng in November 1999, thereby concluding an awkward six-year dispute between Australia and China.[31] Peng was a Chinese-born Australian citizen who had been seized in Macau and convicted and imprisoned in China on embezzlement charges. The Howard Government successfully sidestepped the Taiwan issue in July 1999 by simply refusing to comment when the government of Papua New Guinea, under fiscal limitations, began leaning towards Taiwan to secure alternative finances.[32] It was evident that the Australian Government remained firmly grounded in reality regarding the difficulties of the Australia-China relationship. In 1999 Downer stated:

> We should not succumb to any false notions that we have some kind of 'special' relationship with China. Our government's ground-breaking Foreign and Trade Policy White Paper quite rightly stated that China was one of our four key relationships alongside those with Indonesia, Japan and the United States.[33]

Downer went on to say:

> Instead of some mythical 'special' relationship, what we actually have is a mature and broadly based relationship with China, a relationship

based on mutual respect and mutual advantage. And part of that mature relationship should always be a hard-headed appreciation that China and Australia have both commonalities and differences.[34]

According to Downer, Australia's 'hard-headed' pragmatism, reminiscent of 1996, still remained entrenched in Australia's approach to China.[35]

Irrespective of this pragmatism, by 1999 the cultivation of defence and security ties initiated in 1997 between the two countries had been steadily developing. In 1999 Downer said:

> If we want to discuss security and foreign issues with China in a constructive and informed way, we need a channel into the PLA [People's Liberation Army]. Of course, there are definite limits to how far this cooperation can and should go, but the development of our links with the Chinese military over the last few years has been quite notable. High level visits have underpinned this dialogue. Several senior Chinese officers, including the PLA Chief of General Staff, have visited Australia this year. In May, John Moore became the first ever Australian Defence Minister to visit China, and in October, the Vice Chief of the Australian Defence Force led the Australian side in the third round of our military talks with China.[36]

Even with these security developments, the pre-eminence of 'hard headed' pragmatism reigned supreme in the relationship.[37] The Howard Government recognised that there were 'definite limits to how far this cooperation can and should go'.[38] After the façade of 1996, this maturing pragmatism was rendered transparent on a number of occasions during the period 1997–2002. Tensions in the security domain were exacerbated on 5 May 2000 when Howard, in an interview with Steve Liebmann, controversially linked high-tech Australian Defence Force elements with Taiwan. It appears the Howard Government may have been nervous of Taiwan-China tensions rising after the election of Taiwan pro-independence candidate Chen Shui-ban. In his interview with Howard, Liebmann asked:

> The Commander in Chief of the United States Pacific Command, Admiral Dennis Blair is saying America wants your Government to maintain a high technology Defence Force. Are you prepared to do that at what is implied as a risk to our defence relationship with America if you don't?[39]

Howard responded:

> I don't think he's threatening our defence relationship. I will be seeing Admiral Blair this afternoon. *We do have a high technology Defence Force as far as Taiwan is concerned*, which is the context in which those remarks were made. My message to him this afternoon and indeed to the Chinese

will be to exercise maximum restraint. I don't think we should be talking about the possibility of conflict over Taiwan. I think what we should be doing as a very close ally of the United States, also a country having a constructive relationship with Beijing, is to say to both of them it is in everybody's interests that we all exercise a great deal of restraint. And I'm not going to get into hypothetical situations about what we may and may not do in the event of something happening, I don't think that's helpful.[40]

Although it can be disputed that what Howard meant to say was that Australia has a high-tech force *compared* to that of Taiwan, a cursory glance at the quote would suggest otherwise. Clearly the Howard Government possessed a strong stance towards Chinese military action against Taiwan, and was prepared for such a contingency. This was arguably an even stronger foreign policy position than that assumed in the 1996 Taiwan Strait crisis.

On 1 April 2001 the EP-3 spy plane crisis unfolded between China and the United States, in which a Chinese J-8 fighter jet collided with a US EP-3 reconnaissance aircraft, causing the death of the Chinese pilot and forcing the damaged EP-3 to land on the Chinese island of Hainan. During this tense US–China standoff, Australian naval vessels had an altercation with a Chinese naval vessel in the Taiwan Strait on 17 April 2001. The Australian Defence Force vessels were hailed by a Chinese ship, an action that had never occurred before between the two navies.[41] Despite the extremely tense situation, each country was able to negotiate the stormy period with strong relations intact. Howard persisted in supporting the Australian Defence Force's actions as innocent, despite disagreements with the Chinese Government. Concerning Australia's relationship with China at the time, Howard said:

I don't believe it's shaky at all. China's always had a different view about what international law allows the vessels of one country to do in the territorial waters of another. There's nothing new about that and I don't think we should overreact or exaggerate the significance of what has occurred in the last couple of weeks. The Australian vessels were acting completely in accordance with international law, but equally we don't want to get too sensitive about this. We've got to look at it in the context of an overall relationship which is quite good. In fact much better now than it was a few years ago. And a relationship that *economically* is very important to this country.[42]

A number of important insights can be gleaned from these two statements. Obviously the Howard Government was quite prepared to voice a difference of opinion to that of the Chinese Government. Second, the threat perception of China from 1996 remained strong, as evinced by the high-tech forces statement.

This revealed a rare example of the enduring suspicion of China underneath the Howard Government's positive depictions. While the depiction of China in the two statements was calm and measured, the perception behind the depictions harboured considerable reservations. And decisively, Howard characterised the relationship as economic rather than strategic in nature.

Despite these difficulties, the December 2000 release of Defence's White Paper, *Defence 2000: Our Future Defence Force*, exhibited considerable optimism in the Australian Government's strategic depiction of China. The government stated that 'we believe the forces for peace and stability in the Asia-Pacific region are strong' and 'there is a small but still significant possibility of growing and sustained confrontation between the major powers of Asia'.[43] While a cautionary tone remained palpable, the government recognised the importance of China and the continuation of successful engagement. It stated:

> China, as the country with the fastest growing security influence in the region, is an increasingly important strategic interlocutor for Australia. The Government places a high priority on working with China to deepen and develop our dialogue on strategic issues.[44]

The introduction of the descriptor 'strategic interlocutor' for the first time was an interesting evolution in Australia's depiction of China, possibly conveying the deepening security ties between the two countries. The Defence White Paper stated that 'it is important that Australia take a long term approach to building up our access to those countries strategic thinking, and our influence in their decision making'.[45] By 2000 the strategic dialogue between the two had entered its fourth year. Although the Defence White Paper abstained from discussing China's growing power projection capabilities, it did note that 'a number of regional defence forces have begun to develop sophisticated air combat capabilities'; this of course included China.[46] It also noted that the US-Japan relationship was 'critical to maintaining strategic stability in the region' and that the alliance had 'provided a welcome framework in which Japan has been able to take a larger role in regional and global security issues'.[47] Obviously Japan remained a central facet of Australia's strategic considerations and possible hedging strategy.

To summarise, the period of January 1997 to December 2002 was a period of Australia-China relationship restoration. In 2002 Howard declared:

> We have a closer relationship with China now than we had five years ago. I count it one of the foreign policy achievements of our time in Government so far and that is the development of a strong mutually respectful relationship with China.[48]

The economic relationship moved from strength to strength, growing from A$10.1 billion in 1998–99 to A$22.6 billion in 2002–2003, an annual growth rate of 22 per cent.[49] Strategic and political difficulties remained, but these were successfully navigated with what appeared to be a considerable degree of tolerance after the tensions of 1996. Reminiscing upon the period, Howard mused:

> There are occasions in a reasonably lengthy period of a Prime Ministership when you can look back on particular countries where you feel there has been a quantum shift in the relationship. I certainly had that experience after a visit I paid to Beijing in 1997.[50]

In conclusion, the 1997 DFAT White Paper, 1997 Defence Strategic Review and 2000 Defence White Paper can be regarded as accurate characterisations of the relationship's dynamics during 1997–2002. Economic opportunity and strategic anxiety were yoked together in an uneasy but relatively stable link. The government's strategic depiction of China had remained relatively stable, exhibiting a considerable degree of cooperation and coherence between the depictions made by DFAT and the Department of Defence. The government had begun a deliberately positive strategic depiction of China, in an attempt to allay Chinese fears of strategic isolation. This may have been an early sign of a hedging strategy being implemented by the Howard Government, stating its intent to 'convince Beijing that China's legitimate interests and growing influence can be accommodated within the current regional framework'.[51] Apart from Downer's 'economic strategic partnership' statement in 1997, the government maintained a relatively clear distinction between its economic interest in China and its view of China as a strategic challenge.[52] Policy statements differentiated economic interest from strategic interest. As a result, by 2002 the mood remained remarkably similar to the mood of 1997 and in 1999 when the government declared that it did not have a 'special relationship' with China despite strong trade ties.[53] A considerable degree of angst was observable in the government's strategic depictions of China, noting its growing power projection capabilities. Howard's 2000 high-tech forces statement regarding Taiwan and the 17 April 2001 Taiwan Strait incident clearly showed the serious difficulties persisting in the relationship. In addition, visits to Taiwan by Australian Government officials remained controversial. Important changes had been introduced, especially the bilateral human rights dialogue and the security dialogue. However, the relationship had not assumed an explicit strategic dimension in the Howard Government's public depiction of Australia-China relations. While private accounts indicate that behind the scenes an ongoing strategic dialogue of significant proportions had been underway for a number of years, this remained far from the public eye.[54] Indeed, the period 2003–2006 marks the public declaration of the relationship's strategic evolution that until then remained unannounced. To summarise, the prescient question regarding Australia-China relations at the conclusion of 2002 was, *where to from here*? Having ridden a continuing wave of trade growth while navigating diplomatic disputes with comparative ease relative to the experiences of 1996, commentators were speculating about what future possibilities lay ahead with ongoing friendly relations between Australia and China.[55] And, decisively, in 2003 things were again set to change in how the Howard Government depicted China.

ENDNOTES

[1] Alexander Downer, 'Address to the 1997 Australia in Asia Series', Sydney, 10 September 1997, available at <http://www.dfat.gov.au/media/speeches/foreign/1997/china10sept97.html>, accessed 10 April 2007.

[2] Tim Fischer, 'Address to the Australia–China Forum', Beijing, 8 September 1997, available at <http://www.dfat.gov.au/media/speeches/trade/1997/a-c_forum8sept97.html>, accessed 20 April 2007.

[3] For another example, consider 'strategic economic partnership', first employed by the Howard Government in 2003 (see chapter 3 of this paper).

[4] Alexander Downer, 'Australia and China: A Partnership in Growth', address to launch DFAT's East Asia Analytical Unit's study 'China Embraces the Market: Achievements, Constraints and Opportunities', Sydney, 21 April 1997, available at <http://www.dfat.gov.au/media/speeches/foreign/1997/eaau.html>, accessed 3 April 2007.

[5] Downer, 'Australia and China: A Partnership in Growth'.

[6] Downer, 'Australia and China: A Partnership in Growth'.

[7] The Australia–China Strategic Dialogue was established in 1994 and has occurred approximately annually since 1997. It represents one of China's longest running uninterrupted dialogues of this type—rivalled only by regular talks between the People's Liberation Army and Russia. The Dialogue, which is held alternately in Canberra and Beijing, provides the main coordinating forum for practical aspects of the Australia-China defence relationship, setting the engagement agenda for the following year, as well as a forum for exchanging views on developments in the strategic environment.

[8] Alexander Downer, 'Media release', 10 April 1997, available at <http://www.dfat.gov.au/media/releases/foreign/1997/fa24_97.html>, accessed 10 April 2007.

[9] Downer, 'Australia and China: A Partnership in Growth'.

[10] Department of Foreign Affairs and Trade, *In the National Interest*, Commonwealth of Australia, Canberra, 1997, p. iii.

[11] Department of Foreign Affairs and Trade, *In the National Interest*, p. v.

[12] Department of Foreign Affairs and Trade, *In the National Interest*, p. v.

[13] Department of Foreign Affairs and Trade, *In the National Interest*, p. 29.

[14] Department of Foreign Affairs and Trade, *In the National Interest*, p. 63.

[15] Department of Foreign Affairs and Trade, *In the National Interest*, p. 63.

[16] Department of Defence, *Australia's Strategic Policy: Department of Defence 1997 Strategic Review*, Commonwealth of Australia, Canberra, 1997, p. 14.

[17] Department of Foreign Affairs and Trade, *In the National Interest*, p. v.

[18] Department of Defence, *Australia's Strategic Policy*, p. 14.

[19] Department of Foreign Affairs and Trade, *In the National Interest*, p. 34.

[20] Department of Defence, *Australia's Strategic Policy*, p. 14.

[21] Department of Defence, *Australia's Strategic Policy*, p. 14.

[22] Department of Foreign Affairs and Trade, *In the National Interest*, p. 29.

[23] Department of Defence, *Australia's Strategic Policy*, p. 14.

[24] Department of Defence, *Australia's Strategic Policy*, p. 14.

[25] Department of Defence, *Australia's Strategic Policy*, p. 24. For a comparison, see Department of Foreign Affairs and Trade, *In the National Interest*, p. 63.

[26] Department of Defence, *Australia's Strategic Policy*, p. 14.

[27] Department of Defence, *Australia's Strategic Policy*, p. 14.

[28] *People's Daily Online*, available at <http://english.people.com.cn/zhuanti/Zhuanti_458.html>, accessed 28 November 2008. Informally, hedging can be described as 'spreading one's bets' to reduce risk in a

gambling scenario. For a more formal discussion, see Evelyn Goh, *PacNet*, no. 43, Pacific Forum CSIS, Honolulu, 31 August 2006, available at <http://www.csis.org/media/pubs/pac0643.pdf>, accessed 21 May 2007.

[29] Alexander Downer, 'Australia and Asia—After the Crisis', Occasional Lecture to the Business/Academic Meeting of the Asia Research Centre and the WA State Office of the Department of Foreign Affairs and Trade, Perth, 6 August 1998, available at <http://www.dfat.gov.au/media/speeches/foreign/1998/980806-asia-crisis.html>, accessed 3 April 2007.

[30] Alexander Downer, 'Media release: 10 May 1999', available at <http://www.dfat.gov.au/media/releases/foreign/1999/fa047_99.html>, accessed 16 March 2007.

[31] Alexander Downer, 'Release of James Peng', 14 November 1999, available at <http://www.dfat.gov.au/media/releases/foreign/1999/fa129_99>, accessed 16 March 2007.

[32] John Howard, 'Press conference: Akasaka State Guest House', Tokyo, 6 July 1999, available at <http://www.pm.gov.au/media/interview/1999/akasaka0607.cfm>, accessed 31 March 2007.

[33] Alexander Downer, 'Australia and China—Partners for Progress', address at the 1999 China Oration of the Australia–China Business Council, Sydney, 25 November 1999, available at <http://www.dfat.gov.au/media/speeches/foreign/1999/991125_aust_china.html>, accessed 10 April 2007.

[34] Downer, 'Australia and China—Partners for Progress'.

[35] Alexander Downer, 'Security through Cooperation', address to the International Institute for Strategic Studies/Strategic and Defence Studies Centre Conference, 'The New Security Agenda in the Asia Pacific Region', Canberra, 2 May 1996, available at <http://www.dfat.gov.au/media/speeches/foreign/1996/regsec5.html>, accessed 3 April 2007.

[36] Downer, 'Australia and China—Partners for Progress'.

[37] Downer, 'Security through Cooperation', address to the IISS/SDSC Conference.

[38] Downer, 'Australia and China—Partners for Progress', available at <http://www.dfat.gov.au/media/speeches/foreign/1999/991125_aust_china.html>.

[39] John Howard, 'Interview with Steve Liebmann', 5 May 2000, available at <http://www.pm.gov.au/media/interview/2000/today0505.cfm>, accessed 1 April 2007.

[40] Howard, 'Interview with Steve Liebmann'. [emphasis added]

[41] Jian Zhang, 'Australia and China: Towards a Strategic Partnership?', in James Cotton and John Ravenhill (eds), *Trading on Alliance Security: Australia in World Affairs 2001-2005*, Oxford University Press, Melbourne, 2007, p. 95.

[42] John Howard, 'Interview with Tracy Grimshaw', 30 April 2001, available at <http://www.pm.gov.au/media/interview/2001/interview994.cfm>, accessed 5 March 2007. [emphasis added]

[43] Department of Defence, *Defence 2000: Our Future Defence Force*, 2000 Defence White Paper, Commonwealth of Australia, Canberra, p. 19.

[44] Department of Defence, *Defence 2000: Our Future Defence Force*, p. 37.

[45] Department of Defence, *Defence 2000: Our Future Defence Force*, p. 37.

[46] Department of Defence, *Defence 2000: Our Future Defence Force*, p. 24.

[47] Department of Defence, *Defence 2000: Our Future Defence Force*, p. 18.

[48] John Howard, 'Briefing for Chinese Media', 16 May 2002, Canberra, available at <http://www.pm.gov.au/media/interview/2002/interview1649.cfm>, accessed 28 February 2007.

[49] Australia's total bilateral merchandise trade with China grew from A$10.1 billion in 1998–99 to A$22.6 billion in 2002–2003, an average annual growth of 22 per cent. For the same period, Australia's total merchandise exports to China rose from A$3.9 billion to A$8.8 billion, while its merchandise imports from China increased from A$6.1 billion to A$13.8 billion. See Australian Bureau of Agricultural and Resource Economics, *Trade Flows between Australia and China*, ABARE Conference Paper 05.1, Commonwealth of Australia, Canberra, 2005, available at <http://www.abareconomics.com/publications_html/economy/economy_05/cp05_1.pdf>, accessed 28 November 2008, p. 3.

[50] John Howard, 'Address to Australia India Business Council Lunch', Sydney, 1 September 2006, available at <http://www.pm.gov.au/media/speech/2006/speech2112.cfm>, accessed 17 April 2007.

[51] Department of Defence, *Australia's Strategic Policy*, p. 14.

[52] Alexander Downer, 'Address to the 1997 Australia in Asia Series', Sydney, 10 September 1997, available at <http://www.dfat.gov.au/media/speeches/foreign/1997/china10sept97.html>, accessed 10 April 2007.

[53] Downer, 'Australia and China—Partners for Progress'.

[54] Interview with a former staff member of the Howard Government.

[55] Colin Mackerras, 'Australia–China Relations at the End of the Twentieth Century', *Australian Journal of International Affairs*, vol. 54, no. 2, 2000, p. 198.

Chapter 3

Friendly Unease:
January 2003–December 2006

The Howard Government entered 2003 having presided over one of the most successful periods in the history of Australia-China relations. The period 1997–2002 observed a blooming trade relationship and the successful navigation of intermittent diplomatic disputes. The Howard Government depicted China as an economic partner and strategic interlocutor. Into this positive atmosphere the Department of Foreign Affairs and Trade (DFAT)'s second White Paper *Advancing the National Interest* was launched on 12 February 2003. It proved to be an extremely significant document, for coining one of the most debated phrases in Australia's recent diplomatic history, 'strategic economic partnership', and indicating a new period in Australia-China relations.[1] In contrast to the period 1997–2002, the 2003–2006 period saw the Howard Government depict China as both an economic partner and a strategic partner. However, the controversy surrounding this new strategic partnership forced the government to retreat from publicly acknowledging the strategic relationship. Consequently, the Australia-China relationship during the period can be described as one of 'friendly unease'—'friendly' because of ongoing positive depictions, and 'unease' because of US reactions to Australia's warm depictions of China. This chapter will map these developments, recounting the announcement of the 'strategic relationship' between the two countries and the corresponding strategic shockwave that ensued in Australian foreign policy.[2]

When the Howard Government released the 2003 DFAT White Paper, it heralded the dawn of a new age in Australia-China relations. *Advancing the National Interest* stated: 'The government will pay particular attention to securing the long-term vitality of our successful partnership with Japan and to building a *strategic economic partnership* with China.'[3]

The phrase 'strategic economic partnership' is a perplexing and intriguing one. At first glance the most striking feature of the term is its ambiguity, possibly a deliberate design feature. How does one define the phrase? Does it mean an economic partnership that is of strategic value, or does it infer something more substantial? Could the Howard Government be depicting an economic relationship which is defined primarily by its strategic interests rather than its economic interests?[4] The White Paper went on to say that Australia 'is building a strategic economic relationship with China similar to those Australia has established with Japan and Korea'.[5] This introduces new possibilities for interpretation. Japan and South Korea represent quantifiably substantial relationships with Australia in the strategic realm, particularly Japan. Both countries are important spokes in the US regional 'hub and spokes' bilateral relationship system, and Japan is a key security partner of Australia.[6] Does this mean that Australia's designs for its relationship with China include security cooperation and strategic alignment akin to what it has with Japan and South Korea? Consequently, *Advancing the National Interest* depicted the importance of China in the region, arguably to a position more central in Australia's strategic considerations than Japan. The document stated that 'although much less powerful than Japan on many measures, China's growing economic, political and strategic weight is the single most important trend in the region'.[7] Hence it appeared that the locus of Australia's foreign policy attention in Asia was China, despite Japan's established trade and security ties with Australia.

Advancing the National Interest noted that conflict between the United States and China was possible, stating 'Taiwan will continue to be a potential source of serious tension between the United States and China. The possibility of miscalculation leading to conflict is real, although small'.[8] This was a subtle but significant evolution in the Howard Government's depictions of threats in the Asia-Pacific region. It still noted that the region had security threats, but viewed it as relatively stable. This is to be contrasted with one of the Howard Government's threat depictions of 1996, which identified three areas of concern: Taiwan, the Korean Peninsula and the South China Sea.[9] Indeed, one of the significant developments during the Howard years was the freeze of disputes in the South China Sea, a number of which were based on Chinese claims in the area. In addition, the constructive role of China in the Six-Party Talks appears to have had a significant influence on the Howard Government's perception of China, and its corresponding strategic depiction.[10] However, not all of the Howard Government's departments possessed such a uniformly positive depiction of the relationship. In mild contrast, *Defence Update 2003* predicted continuing strategic competition between the United States and China, especially concerning Taiwan; 'strategic competition between the United States and China will continue over the next decade, and the possibility of miscalculation over Taiwan persists'.[11] It went on to state:

> China, as the country with the fastest growing security influence in the region, is an increasingly important strategic interlocutor for Australia. The Government places a high priority on working with China to deepen and develop our dialogue on strategic issues.[12]

The phrase 'strategic interlocutor', first employed in the Defence White Paper 2000, reinforced the Howard Government's depiction of China as a recognised and significant strategic player in the region. And on 13 August 2004, John

Howard used 'strategic economic relationship' for the first time in a public speech.[13]

Having consolidated the use of 'strategic economic relationship' in public debate, Howard and Alexander Downer began to increasingly depict Australia as a mediator between the United States and China:

> Our aim is to see calm and constructive dialogue between the United States and China. The government recognises that, as a nation which has different but nonetheless close relationships with both countries, Australia is well placed to promote that constructive dialogue.[14]

On the same day as Howard, Downer made a significant speech to the Australia–China Free Trade Agreement Conference, emphasising the importance of China in the region. Downer said China had 'cemented its role as a constructive actor and a valued contributor to the region's core security and stability'.[15] On a new tangent, Downer praised China as a 'good friend' who was playing a positive role in Iraq:

> China has played a crucial role in helping advance the international response to Iraq over the past few months, ensuring that Security Council Resolution 1546 was unanimously adopted and clearly signalling its support for the new Iraqi government and an active role for the international community.[16]

These statements represent important evolutions in Australia's strategic depiction of China. Australian foreign policy was beginning to recognise the broader role of China in the United Nations and global security. Downer went on to say:

> We see considerable opportunity for further cooperation with China as we continue to build and strengthen regional security with China's ongoing role as a positive force in the region as crucial to our interests as it is to China's. It is therefore fitting that we have developed annual bilateral dialogues on regional security and defence issues.[17]

In addition to deepening defence and security ties, new economic initiatives were being developed too. Concerning the negotiation of a Free Trade Agreement Downer said:

> The Government recognises that the current strengths of the relationship make this an opportune time to look at a possible FTA [Free Trade Agreement] with China and that an FTA would lend important strategic support to our efforts to build and strengthen the broader bilateral relationship in the future.[18]

This was again a tantalising depiction of China by Australia. Was the relationship purely economic? Clearly the notion of a Free Trade Agreement providing 'important strategic support' to the crafting of a 'broader bilateral relationship' is provocative. But was this a depiction of a genuine strategic relationship? Downer went on to say:

> I hope that my remarks will also assist the conference in their consideration of the significant role China plays, not just in terms of trade and economic interests, but issues that relate to the security and prosperity of our region.[19]

Again, Downer refrained from making a full blown 'strategic relationship' reference, but the mood of the text is enticing. By themselves the statements are ground-breaking in their acceptance and support for China's greater role in regional and global strategy and security. The government had affirmed China as a 'good friend' who was a 'positive force' in the Asia-Pacific region, playing the role of a 'strategic interlocutor' in regional and global affairs such as Iraq.[20]

Having noted these remarkably warm strategic depictions of China by Howard and Downer on 13 August 2004, it is compelling to introduce Downer's statements made in Beijing only four days later. On 17 August 2004, while visiting China, Downer made one of the most talked about statements in recent times regarding Australia-China relations. Downer said in Beijing:

> With Premier Wen we agreed that Australia and China would build up a bilateral *strategic relationship*, that we would strengthen our economic relationship and we would work together closely on Asia Pacific issues, be they economic or security issues.[21]

This was a ground-breaking statement. Previously in the Howard Government's strategic depiction of China there had been a steady evolution in the relationship, from an economic relationship, to an economic relationship with strategic significance, to a 'strategic economic relationship'.[22] And now the transition appeared complete, Australia and China had established an explicit 'strategic relationship'.[23] However, this was not the only change. In response to a carefully constructed question by the media regarding Taiwan, Downer went on to say:

> Well, the ANZUS Treaty is a treaty which of course is symbolic of the Australian alliance relationship with the United States, but the ANZUS Treaty is invoked in the event of one of our two countries, Australia or the United States, being attacked. So other military activity elsewhere in the world, be it in Iraq or anywhere else for that matter does not automatically invoke the ANZUS Treaty.[24]

This was a fundamental reinterpretation of the ANZUS alliance, reassessing its core commitment of consultation in the case of alliance forces being attacked. The ANZUS alliance had been reduced to a largely symbolic alliance, invoked in the instance of attacks upon the American or Australian homeland as in the case of the 11 September 2001 terrorist attacks on the United States. This was obviously a significant reduction of the alliance commitment, away from the more comprehensive and orthodox ANZUS forces interpretation. But Downer had not finished. He went on to say:

> Diplomatic relations between countries evolve, you know, rather than change by gigantic steps—and what we are seeing through what Premier Wen said to me about building a strategic relationship between Australia and China is a significant development, in that I think China has seen Australia in years gone by as an important economic partner and a less important political and strategic partner, and I think now there is a recognition by the Chinese leadership of the significant role that Australia plays in the region.[25]

If the point had not been made before, now it was glaringly obvious. Far from being a slip of the tongue, for the second time Downer had confirmed that Australia and China did indeed have a strategic relationship. Downer went on to say: 'I think we are seeing the evolution of a much stronger and much fuller relationship which encompasses many challenges of the Asia-Pacific region of the political and security nature, not just of an economic nature.'[26] Having ascended to the heights of reinterpreting the ANZUS alliance, Downer had plainly described a 'strategic relationship' between Australia and China for the first time in history.[27] The statements came hand in hand: a reduction of ANZUS to a highly symbolic status, coupled with a fundamental reorientation of Australia's strategic posture towards China. What occurred over the next few days was a curious flurry of back-peddling as Howard and Downer tried to recant the statement. The Australian domestic and American response was noisy and raucous as the strategic shockwave spread.[28] A few days later Howard responded that 'nobody can doubt that Australia is a loyal ally of the United States', and reverted to the orthodox interpretation of ANZUS as being invoked in an attack on ANZUS forces.[29]

By March 2005 it appeared that Howard was still attempting to heal the US-Australia relationship. He reinforced the closeness of US-Australia ties, but this was juggled with maintenance of the Australia-China relationship. Howard highlighted the differences and similarities between Australia and China. He said:

> Now everybody knows that Australia has no closer ally than the United States, now that is a given of our foreign policy, it's a given of so many aspects of Australian life, everybody knows also that we have developed

a good relationship with China, we are different countries. China is not a democracy, Australia is, there are a lot of things in China that we don't agree with, equally however, we have very strong people to people links and we will work very hard to further expand that relationship. So it's in our interests to work at preventing anything from occurring and I am not going to start hypothesising about how we would react if those efforts were to fail, there is nothing to be achieved by that.[30]

Apparently the normative response of the period 1997–2002 was back in vogue; that Australia had close but different relations with the United States and China, and the government was not going to hypothesise about its response to a Taiwan contingency. However, a landmark speech by Howard to the Sydney-based Lowy Institute for International Policy in March 2005 again signalled Australia's new depiction of China in the region. It appeared that the integration of China into Australia's strategic posture was back on the agenda. Regarding US-China relations Howard said: 'It would be a mistake to embrace an overly pessimistic view of this relationship, pointing to unavoidable conflict. Australia does not believe that there is anything inevitable about escalating strategic competition between China and the US.'[31]

Howard's Lowy Institute address reveals that Australian and US perspectives on China were becoming divergent. At the 2005 IISS Shangri-La Dialogue in Singapore, the contrasting regional defence interests of Australia and the United States were again clearly displayed. While US Secretary of Defense Donald Rumsfeld spoke of China's growing missile capabilities, Australian Defence Minister Robert Hill's address remained focused on countering terrorism.[32] Although Rumsfeld briefly mentioned terrorism, Hill did not mention China once. Hill's exclusion of China and missile defence was an important shift away from the Defence 2000 White Paper, which had discussed both.[33]

When George W. Bush and John Howard stood side by side conducting a joint press conference on the White House lawn on 19 July 2005 these differences were again plain to see. While Bush's strategic depiction of China was characterised by an emphasis upon the sensitivities in the US-China relationship, Howard took a friendlier tone, emphasising the challenges and successes of Australia-China relations. Bush began by noting 'one such difficulty is their currency, and we've worked with China to convince them it makes sense for the Chinese, to change how they value their currency'.[34] He then observed that 'a second difficulty is on intellectual property rights. It's very important for emerging economies to understand that they—in order to be a fair trading partner, that you've got to honor somebody else's intellectual property'.[35] Bush then asserted 'we've got areas of issues when it comes to values. For example, I happen to believe religious freedom is very important'.[36] He concluded by remarking that 'our relationship is very important and very vibrant. It's a good relationship, but it's a complex relationship'.[37] In contrast, Howard's remarks were far more conciliatory, focusing on the positives in the relationship. First of all Howard began by reinforcing the Australia-US relationship. He said:

> We have different relationships with the United States and China. I mean, of course, our relationship with the United States is closer and deeper than it is with China, because it's a relationship that is based upon shared values and a lot of shared history. The Chinese understand that. I think one of the bases—the basis of our relationship successfully with China over the last eight or nine years—is that I have never disguised that fact in my discussion with the Chinese, and I've encouraged them to accept that our close defence alliance with the United States is not in any way directed against China.[38]

The question is, was this a message to the Chinese or the Americans? Howard went on to say:

> But we have a good relationship with China. It's not just based on economic opportunity. There are a lot of people-to-people ties between Australia and China, and they're growing all the time. We are going to differ with China on human rights issues. You've seen recently, in the debate over Mr. Chen, you've seen an expression of views from China. But equally, I think the relationship between our two countries is mature enough to ride through temporary arguments such as that. I think China sees a growing place for herself in the world, but I think there's a great level of pragmatism in the Chinese leadership. Now, the economic relationship between Australia and China is different from the economic relationship between the United States and China. And I understand that and the President and I talked about that today.[39]

Howard was quick to emphasise the enduring stability of the Australia-China relationship. Despite the recent Chen debacle, an embarrassing incident that could have gone awry, the two governments were proving to be adroit at navigating around these kinds of issues.[40] And again, the Howard Government appeared to be alluding to much more when it said that it had a different economic relationship with China compared to the US-China trade relationship.

In 2003 the Howard Government had announced the cultivation of a 'strategic economic relationship' between Australia and China, but no comparative phrase had been utilised to describe Australia-US trade relations.[41] Hence the subtleties of diplomatic speech were again apparent—the Howard Government was arguably attempting to convey that its relationship with China constituted more than mere economic interest, without making a 'strategic relationship' statement that would arouse US disapproval. Having discussed the limitation of ANZUS ('our close defence alliance with the United States is not in any way directed against China'), it seemed that Howard was now reiterating that Australia's economic relationship with China could not be defined solely as the pursuit of economic interest.[42] Howard then progressed to say:

> But I have a more optimistic view about the relationship between China and the United States, and I know the leadership of both countries understand the importance of commonsense in relation to Taiwan, recognition that there are differences of philosophy between the two societies.[43]

As often announced in the past, Howard desired to see a peaceful and stable US-China relationship in regards to Taiwan, and maintained a positive view of that relationship. Howard continued to reinforce this positive view, saying:

> But let us not look at this issue from an Australian vantage point of believing that there's some inevitable dust-up going to occur. I don't believe that, and I share a great deal of optimism that this is going to be prevented. From Australia's point of view, well, we don't presume any kind of intermediary role. That would be absurd.[44]

Arguably the most interesting development in the direction of Australian foreign policy revealed by this Bush/Howard joint press release was Australia's decline from playing an intermediary role in the US-China relationship (the fact that it is unlikely the United States and China ever viewed Australia as an intermediary is inconsequential). In previous statements the Howard Government appeared to be grooming itself as a self-styled mediator between the two countries.[45] Clearly this mediating role was now out of the question.

In summary, a number of points stand out from this meeting. First, the US-Australia relationship was allegedly rock solid. Second, Australia had good relations with both the United States and China. Third, these relations were positive yet different at the same time. Fourth, Australia had an optimistic view of the region's future. Fifth, Australia was not an intermediary between the United States and China. And sixth, ANZUS was not directed against China. These policy statements had all been reiterated and reinforced after Downer's August 2004 Beijing statement. It appears that the Howard Government was temporarily stunned from the Beijing affair and resorted to reaffirming policy previously employed during 1997–2002. Australia's rejection of mediating between the United States and China seems to have been an instinctive response to the controversy caused by Downer's statement. Despite these difficult developments in the Australia–US–China triangle, the Howard Government remained optimistic.

In August 2005 Downer delivered a landmark address, the Tange lecture, again indicating a warming of Australia's view towards China's growing strategic influence in the region. Downer said: 'The argument that Australia needs to choose definitively between its alliance with the United States and its links with China also misjudges the nature of Australia's relationship with each of these countries.'[46] Although Downer said Australia approached China with a 'spirit of ambition without illusions', the persistently positive strategic depiction of China remained.[47] He said: 'We see a confident, peaceful and prosperous China, with an open market economy and constructively engaged in global and regional institutions, as an enormous asset for the Asia-Pacific region and the wider world.'[48]

Even though Downer's statement can be qualified as an ideal characterisation of China in the future, other Australian Government publications such as the 2005 *Defence Update* reiterated this positive theme. China's 'peaceful development' had become the accepted policy line on China's rise. It stated that 'China's interests lie in a secure, stable flow of resources to support its economic modernisation, and the development of markets for its goods and services'.[49] Likewise, in September 2005, Howard said 'to see China's rise in zero sum terms is overly pessimistic, intellectually misguided and potentially dangerous'.[50]

The preceding statements are significant for exemplifying what Michael Wesley has described as the Howard Government's 'hope based formula' of dual engagement with the United States and China.[51] The Howard Government believed it could have friendly relations with the United States and China, and separate itself from US-China tensions at the same time. Building upon Downer's Tange lecture, the then Australian Ambassador to the United States, Dennis Richardson, in January 2006 described China's rise as a positive process. He stated that 'the question for Australia is not whether China's growth is innately good or bad. Australia made up its mind long ago that it was a good thing'.[52] Richardson also acknowledged that China's military modernisation was advancing at rapid pace, but he believed these developments were not necessarily aggressive. He argued:

> The question, rather, is to what extent China's rise will change the system in which it rises. Can it play by the rules or will it change the rules? We in Australia want China to play by the rules, just as Australia, Japan or others do, and we have every reason to believe that it will do so.[53]

What were Richardson's reasons for believing China would behave responsibly within the Asia-Pacific system? The AusAID White Paper of 2006 offers a number of clues. It discussed the emergence of India and China's 'strategic footprint' in the Asia-Pacific region, with particular reference to aid programs.[54] *Promoting Growth and Stability* announced: 'China continues to look outwards and, apart from its growing political and economic influence, is emerging as a significant donor to the region (it is among the largest bilateral donors to the Pacific).'[55]

Thus, the impact of Chinese aid in the region was apparently reaping significant rewards in reforming China's regional image. AusAID recognised China as a 'significant power' that was 'asserting her legitimate interest', and also alluded to China increasingly performing a lead role in the region's aid programs, stating 'Australia will also seek opportunities for cooperation with China in the Pacific, as China's regional aid presence is now significant and growing'.[56] These statements indicated increasing recognition within the organisations of the Howard Government of China's strategic weight in the Asia-Pacific region. But would China use its new-found power to integrate with the Asia-Pacific system or alter it? At the same time, it can be argued that AusAID probably held significant reservations about China's effect on stability in the region.[57] Concerning China's present behaviour, Howard said:

> China has an interest in stable acceptance, not only in the region but in the world because that's crucial to her economic growth. I mean China's preoccupation at the moment is economic growth and expansion and also dealing with the rather growing divide between the coastal affluent and the not so affluent people who live in the rural areas of the country. So there are domestic issues that will keep China's focus very much on economic, rather than military matters.[58]

Consequently, in Howard's mind, China's strategic challenge *for the moment* had been decisively negated by its dependency upon stable economic conditions for continuing economic growth. Confirming what Ambassador Richardson had noted six months earlier, Australia had reason to trust China's rise. Howard's statement appeared to signal a clear end to an internal policy debate concerning Australia's depiction of China's rise. As far back as 1996 the Howard Government had recognised that China's economic rise was a source of potential strategic instability in the Asia-Pacific region.[59] China's growing economy was enabling it to develop its military capabilities at rapid pace. A decade later, Howard for the first time publicly articulated his rationale for confidence in China's peaceful development and his 'hope based formula'.[60] China was chained by its own appetite to acting responsibly in the regional and global polity. The rising power, although developing its military capabilities at a notable rate, would be restrained from flexing its military muscle due to economic interests.

Yet the tide of pro-China rhetoric was not unequivocal. Although Howard continued to praise China's regional role, other policy initiatives were subtly coming into sight. In September 2005 Howard said 'no relationship of substance in Asia has been more important over the years for Australia than our relationship with Japan'.[61] This was a new development. Although Japan had always warranted mention in the Howard Government's discussions regarding Asia, this statement appeared to represent a new strand of policy coming to the fore. Previously in 1997 the Howard Government had commented that 'Japan's strategic interests converge quite strongly with Australia's'.[62] Also adopting a view similar to those expressed in 1997, the 2005 *Defence Update* assumed a more cautionary tone towards China. Sounding similar to the 1997 Strategic Review, the Defence report stated that 'the pace and scale of China's defence modernisation may create the potential for misunderstandings, particularly with the development of new military strike capabilities that extend the strike capability and sustainability of its forces'.[63] This statement is reminiscent of the 1997 Strategic Review, again acknowledging China's growing power projection capabilities. Was this the resurfacing and depiction of threat perceptions from 1997?

To summarise, by 2006 Australia had conducted a radical evolution in its relationship with China. In April 2006, while meeting with Chinese Premier Wen Jiabao in Canberra, Prime Minister John Howard acknowledged that:

> Of all the relationships that Australia has, major relationships it [*sic*] has with other countries, none has been more completely transformed than the relationship with China over the last ten years. Now I don't seek to invoke language such as special relationships and so forth, but I simply make the point that the transformation of the relationship with China has been remarkable.[64]

Evidently a remarkable transition in the mood of Australia-China relations had occurred from 1996–2006. This was not limited to strategic depictions. Howard's personal diplomacy had advanced from the low point of his office—a crisis meeting with Jiang Zemin in Manila in 1996—to the intimate honour of 'jogging diplomacy' with Chinese Premier Wen Jiabao on the banks of Lake Burley Griffin, Canberra, in April 2006. As the Chinese embassy noted, Premier Wen 'was the first foreign leader he [Howard] walked with in the early morning and that it was a major breakthrough in Australia–China relations'.[65]

Although the United States remained central to Australian strategic considerations at the same time, Howard was at pains to point out that in Australia 'we do come at China from a slightly different perspective and I think in that way we can, I guess, be of assistance with the views we offer on China'.[66]

Consequently, the period 2003–2006 is one of the most interesting and perplexing of the Howard Government's time in office. A clear sense of 'friendly unease' can be ascertained from the mood of the Howard Government's rhetoric concerning China. The government signalled the arrival of the new period with the 2003 DFAT White Paper's declaration of a 'strategic economic partnership'.[67] This ambiguous phrase possibly highlighted a new era of strategic transition occurring within Australian foreign policy. While Australia's economic interests remained central, continued exchanges between the militaries of Australia and China set Australia's engagement with China apart from other US friends in the region.[68] Within this context, Downer's 2004 'strategic relationship' statement in Beijing sent a strategic shockwave throughout the Australian and American community. The remaining years observed Australia struggling to harmonise its ANZUS commitment with its growing engagement with China. When Howard and Bush stood side by side on the White House lawn in July 2005, it was apparent to Australia and the world that Australia's depiction of China had diverged considerably from that of the United States. Despite Australia's interests in a stable US-China relationship and Asia-Pacific region, it had growing reservations about being embroiled in disputes between the two countries. However, the Howard Government's depictions remained positive regarding the future, arguing that China's economic interests would restrain China from exercising its growing military capabilities. By the end of 2006, the Australia-China relationship stood in a position of strategic uncertainty. The two countries had drawn closer together than ever before, especially in the trade domain.[69] But the costs in regards to relations with the United States were beginning to become apparent. Australia's deepening relationship with China has not gone unnoticed in Washington. The September 2005 US–China Economic and Security Review Commission's report commented, 'regrettably, the Downer statement is not an isolated case' (in reference to Downer in Beijing 2004), and further noted that 'to these rhetorical shifts can be added shifts in the Australian position on key issues of concern to Washington'.[70] How the Howard Government would respond to growing US reservations remained unseen.

ENDNOTES

[1] Department of Foreign Affairs and Trade, *Advancing the National Interest*, Australia's Foreign and Trade Policy White Paper, Canberra, 2003, p. xv.

[2] Alexander Downer, 'Media Conference: 17 August 2004', Beijing, available at <http://www.foreignminister.gov.au/transcripts/2004/040817_ds_beijing.html>, accessed 2 April 2007.

[3] Department of Foreign Affairs and Trade, *Advancing the National Interest*, p. xv. [emphasis added].

[4] Discussing and defining 'strategic economic relationship' can inspire lively debate, and remains wrought with difficulty. One commentator's valued response to this investigation stated: 'The author seems to avoid the most literal interpretation—that Australia's economic relationship with China seemed destined to be of such consequence as to warrant the label "strategic" but that the DFAT Paper sought to distinguish (rather than blend) this prospect from Australia's strategic security orientation.'

[5] Department of Foreign Affairs and Trade, *Advancing the National Interest*, p. 79.

[6] Kent E. Calder, 'Securing security through prosperity: the San Francisco System in comparative perspective', *The Pacific Review*, vol. 17, no. 1, March 2004, p. 139.

[7] Department of Foreign Affairs and Trade, *Advancing the National Interest*, p. 22.

[8] Department of Foreign Affairs and Trade, *Advancing the National Interest*, p. 22.

[9] Alexander Downer, 'Regional Cooperation and Security', address to the Australian College of Defence and Strategic Studies, Canberra, 6 December 1996, available at <http://www.dfat.gov.au/media/speeches/foreign/1996/regional_coop_security.html>, accessed 2 April 2007.

[10] Alexander Downer, 'Australia and China's Shared Interests—Security and Strategic Dimensions', Speech to the Australia–China Free Trade Agreement Conference, Sydney, 13 August 2004, available at <http://www.foreignminister.gov.au/speeches/2004/040813_aus_china_fta.html>, accessed 2 April 2007.

[11] Department of Defence, *Australia's National Security: A Defence Update 2003*, Commonwealth of Australia, Canberra, p. 8.

[12] Department of Defence, *Australia's National Security: A Defence Update 2003*, p. 8.

[13] John Howard, 'Address to the Asialink—ANU National Forum: Australia's Engagement with Asia: A New Paradigm', Canberra, 13 August 2004, available at <http://www.pm.gov.au/media/speech/2004/speech1069.cfm>, accessed 5 March 2007.

[14] Howard, 'Australia's Engagement with Asia: A New Paradigm'.

[15] Downer, 'Australia and China's Shared Interests—Security and Strategic Dimensions'.

[16] Downer, 'Australia and China's Shared Interests—Security and Strategic Dimensions'.

[17] Downer, 'Australia and China's Shared Interests—Security and Strategic Dimensions'.

[18] Downer, 'Australia and China's Shared Interests—Security and Strategic Dimensions'.

[19] Downer, 'Australia and China's Shared Interests—Security and Strategic Dimensions'.

[20] Downer, 'Australia and China's Shared Interests—Security and Strategic Dimensions'.

[21] Alexander Downer, 'Media Conference: 17 August 2004', Beijing, available at <http://www.foreignminister.gov.au/transcripts/2004/040817_ds_beijing.html>, accessed 2 April 2007. [emphasis added]

[22] Department of Foreign Affairs and Trade, *Advancing the National Interest*, p. 79.

[23] Downer, 'Media Conference', 17 August 2004.

[24] Downer, 'Media Conference', 17 August 2004.

[25] Downer, 'Media Conference', 17 August 2004.

[26] Downer, 'Media Conference', 17 August 2004.

[27] Downer, 'Media Conference', 17 August 2004.

[28] Greg Sheridan, 'Taiwan gaffe puts delicate balance at risk', *Australian*, 21 August 2004, p. 31.

[29] John Howard, 'Interview with Neil Mitchell', 20 August 2004, available at <http://www.pm.gov.au/media/interview/2004/Interview1086.cfm>, accessed 31 March 2007.

[30] John Howard, 'Interview with John Miller and Ross Davie', 15 March 2005, Brisbane, available at <http://www.pm.gov.au/media/interview/2005/Interview 1273.cfm>, accessed 1 April 2007.

[31] John Howard, 'Australia in the World', address to the Lowy Institute for International Policy, Sydney, 31 March 2005, available at <http://www.lowyinstitute.org/Publication.asp?pid=396>, accessed 28 November 2008.

[32] Donald Rumsfeld, US Secretary of Defense, First Plenary Session, The IISS Shangri-La Dialogue, Singapore, 4 June 2005, available at <http://www.iiss.org/conferences/the-shangri-la-dialogue/shangri-la-dialogue-2005/2005-speeches/first-plenary-session-the-hon-donald-rumsfeld>, accessed 7 May 2007; and Senator Robert Hill, Australia Minister of Defence, Fourth Plenary Session, The IISS Shangri-La Dialogue, Singapore, 5 June 2005, available at <http://www.iiss.org/conferences/the-shangri-la-dialogue/shangri-la-dialogue-2005/2005-speeches/fourth-plenary-session-the-hon-robert-hill>, accessed 7 May 2007.

[33] For discussion of China in the *Defence 2000* White Paper, see Department of Defence, *Defence 2000: Our Future Defence Force*, 2000 Defence White Paper, Commonwealth of Australia, Canberra, p. 37. For discussion of ballistic missiles in the *Defence 2000* White Paper, see Department of Defence, *Defence 2000: Our Future Defence Force*, p. 23.

[34] John Howard, 'Joint Press Conference with the President of the United States of America George W Bush', Washington, DC, 19 July 2005, available at <http://www.pm.gov.au/media/interview/2005/Interview1472.cfm>, accessed 28 February 2007.

[35] Howard, 'Joint Press Conference with the President of the United States of America George W Bush'.

[36] Howard, 'Joint Press Conference with the President of the United States of America George W Bush'.

[37] Howard, 'Joint Press Conference with the President of the United States of America George W Bush'.

[38] Howard, 'Joint Press Conference with the President of the United States of America George W Bush'.

[39] Howard, 'Joint Press Conference with the President of the United States of America George W Bush'.

[40] Chen Yonglin was a first secretary for political affairs in the Chinese Consulate-General in Sydney. Prior to his posting, Yonglin had been a political dissident associated with the pro-democracy movement in China. On 26 May 2005 he defected, applying for political asylum in Australia. Yonglin's defection

caused considerable embarrassment and awkwardness, Yonglin claiming that more than 1000 Chinese spies operated in Australia. The debacle was eventually resolved by Australia granting Yonglin a special protection visa rather than full-fledged political asylum. See Zhang Jian, 'Australia and China: Towards a Strategic Partnership?', in James Cotton and John Ravenhill (eds), *Trading on Alliance Security: Australia in World Affairs 2001-2005*, Oxford University Press, Melbourne, 2007, p. 100.

[41] Department of Foreign Affairs and Trade, *Advancing the National Interest*, p. 79.

[42] Howard, 'Joint Press Conference with the President of the United States of America George W Bush'.

[43] Howard, 'Joint Press Conference with the President of the United States of America George W Bush'.

[44] Howard, 'Joint Press Conference with the President of the United States of America George W Bush'.

[45] As mentioned previously, Howard had said in 2004: 'Our aim is to see calm and constructive dialogue between the United States and China. The government recognises that, as a nation which has different but nonetheless close relationships with both countries, Australia is well placed to promote that constructive dialogue.' See Howard, 'Australia's Engagement with Asia: A New Paradigm', available at <http://www.pm.gov.au/media/speech/2004/speech1069.cfm>, accessed 5 March 2007.

[46] Alexander Downer, 'Biennial Sir Arthur Tange Lecture in Australian Diplomacy', Canberra, 8 August 2005, available at <http://www.foreignminister.gov.au/speeches/2005/050808_tange.html>, accessed 26 February 2007.

[47] Downer, 'Biennial Sir Arthur Tange Lecture in Australian Diplomacy'.

[48] Downer, 'Biennial Sir Arthur Tange Lecture in Australian Diplomacy'.

[49] Department of Defence, *Australia's National Security: A Defence Update 2005*, Commonwealth of Australia, Canberra, 2005, available at <http://www.defence.gov.au/update2005/defence_update_2005.pdf>, accessed 28 November 2008.

[50] John Howard, 'Australian Outlook: Australian Policy Priorities for the Asia Pacific', address to the Asia Society, New York, 12 September 2005, available at <http://www.asiasociety.org.au/speeches/speeches_current/s42_John_Howard_NY.htm>, accessed 28 November 2008.

[51] Michael Wesley, *The Howard Paradox: Australian Diplomacy in Asia from 1996-2006*, ABC Books, Sydney, 2007 p. 218.

[52] Australian Ambassador to the United States Dennis Richardson, 'Address at the Brookings Institution', Washington, DC, 24 January 2006, available at <http://www.austemb.org/whwh/SpeechEAsia.html>, accessed 6 May 2007.

[53] Richardson, 'Address at the Brookings Institution'.

[54] AusAid, *Promoting Growth and Stability, A White Paper on the Australian Government's Overseas Aid Program*, April 2006, Commonwealth of Australia, Canberra, p. xi, available at <http://www.ausaid.gov.au/publications/pdf/whitepaper.pdf>, accessed 28 November 2008.

[55] AusAid, *Promoting Growth and Stability*, p. 13.

[56] AusAid, *Promoting Growth and Stability*, p. 28.

[57] In 2006 instability in the Solomon Islands was sparked in part by rivalry between China and Taiwan. See Graeme Dobell, 'China and Taiwan in the South Pacific: Diplomatic Chess versus Pacific Political Rugby', *Policy Brief*, The Lowy Institute for International Policy, Sydney, January 2007.

[58] John Howard, 'Interview with David Speers', Batam, Indonesia, available at <http://www.pm.gov.au/media/interview/2006/Interview1997.cfm>, accessed 6 April 2007.

[59] Alexander Downer, address to the International Institute for Strategic Studies/Strategic and Defence Studies Centre Conference, 'The New Security Agenda in the Asia Pacific Region', available at <http://www.dfat.gov.au/media/speeches/foreign/1996/regsec5.html>, accessed 3 April 2007.

[60] Wesley, *The Howard Paradox: Australian Diplomacy in Asia 1996-2006*, p. 218.

[61] Howard, 'Australian Outlook: Australian Policy Priorities for the Asia Pacific'.

[62] Department of Defence, *Australia's Strategic Policy: Department of Defence 1997 Strategic Review*, Commonwealth of Australia, Canberra, 1997, p. 24.

[63] Department of Defence, *Australia's National Security: A Defence Update 2005*, p. 6.

[64] John Howard, 'Joint Press Conference with His Excellency Mr Wen Jiabao, Premier of the State Council, People's Republic of China', 3 April 2006, Canberra, available at <http://www.pm.gov.au/media/interview/2006/Interview1854.cfm>, accessed 28 February 2007.

[65] 'Premier Wen Jiabao's Visit and China–Australia Relations', Embassy of the People's Republic of China in Australia, April 2006, available at <http://au.china-embassy.org/eng/sgjs/sghd/t247388.htm>, accessed 28 November 2008.

[66] Howard, 'Interview with David Speers'.

[67] Department of Foreign Affairs and Trade, *Advancing the National Interest*, p. xv.

[68] Forty-one senior military exchanges occurred between 2001 and 2004. Australian Defence Ministers visited China in 2001, 2003 and 2005. In October 2004 HMAS *ANZAC* visited Qingdao port and participated in a five-day joint search and rescue drill with the People's Liberation Army Navy. This made Australia one of the few Western countries to conduct joint exercises with China. See Zhang Jian, 'Australia and China: Towards a Strategic Partnership?', in James Cotton and John Ravenhill (eds), *Trading on Alliance Security: Australia in World Affairs 2001-2005*, Oxford University Press, Melbourne, 2007, p. 107.

[69] In the financial year 2005/2006, exports to China surged by 87 per cent to A$8.3 billion. See Department of Foreign Affairs and Trade, *Trade 2006*, Commonwealth of Australia, Canberra, 2006, p. 13.

[70] 'China's Military Modernization and Cross-Strait Balance', hearing before the US–China Economic and Security Review Commission, One Hundred Ninth Congress, First Session, 15 September 2005, p. 232.

Conclusion

As the 2005 US–China Economic and Security Review Commission's report demonstrates, Australia's depiction of China has an influence on regional strategy.[1] Studying the Howard Government's depiction of China during the 1996–2006 period is important for gaining insight into how Australia may manage its dual interests of security (United States) and prosperity (China) in future. The Howard Government's relatively successful management of this potentially volatile conflict of interest sets an important model to consider when deliberating Australian policy towards China. With the Rudd Government posturing towards innovation in its strategic depiction of China, it remains to be seen whether the Howard Government's strategic depiction of China will have a lasting influence on Australia-China relations.

The focus of this paper has sought to ascertain whether Michael Wesley's 'hope based formula' and Paul Kelly's 'response agent' were accurate descriptions of Howard Government depictions of China at the time, or whether a more complex and coherent policy of depictions was implemented.

In the first period, 1996, it is clear that the Australian Government had no chance to implement an effective policy towards China; it was in crisis management mode throughout the year as multiple controversies broke out. Kelly's portrayal of Howard as a 'response agent' is fairly accurate; however the government did announce a future strategy of 'practical bilateralism' to engage China, and depicted the region's security environment as 'benign'.[2]

The 1997–2002 period shows the Howard Government playing a more creative role in its depictions of China. Trade relations assumed a momentum of their own and the government was happy to report these positive developments. These events display the government as a 'response agent' again, riding the wave of economic fortune. However, other policy depictions reveal that strategic concerns still remained. In particular, the 1997 Strategic Review and the Defence 2000 White Paper put forth considered and cautious statements about China's rise. John Howard's 2000 high-tech Australian Defence Force statement and the 2001 Taiwan Strait incident between Australian and Chinese naval vessels also revealed that serious problems persisted. That the Howard Government tended to marginalise the tensions apparent in US-China relations, and Australia-China relations, lends support to Wesley's description of Howard Government policy towards China being conducted according to a 'hope based formula'.[3]

The 2003–2006 period is therefore the most intriguing, revealing the Howard Government actively trying to cultivate its positive depiction of China. Kelly's 'response agent' and Wesley's 'hope based formula' become less accurate descriptions for this period. A common judgement from this period is that

Howard Government statements exhibit considerable Sinofication. However, other Howard Government statements continued to convey strategic caution. The question is, why the change in this period, towards depicting a 'strategic relationship' between Australia and China?[4] The 2003 strategic environment was remarkably similar to 2002. It appears that the 2003 Department of Foreign Affairs and Trade White Paper was a deliberate attempt to change how China and the United States believed Australia was viewing China. Downer's statements in Beijing the next year are even more provocative. The diplomatic fallout from Alexander Downer's Beijing statement amounts to crisis management rather than a policy reversal from what Downer originally said. After the considered 'strategic economic relationship' statement of 2003, Downer's Beijing comments appear rushed and poorly conceived, exhibiting a lack of strategic poise, rather than a sound exposition of strategic policy.[5] Despite this poor delivery, the remaining timeframe from August 2004 to December 2006 charts the government's consolidation of the 'strategic relationship' statement, through speeches such as Downer's Tange Lecture and Howard's Lowy Institute for International Policy address, while beginning to build up other aspects of Australia's hedging strategy. Although the government refrained from employing the phrase 'strategic relationship', the warm overtures towards China were apparent.[6]

To summarise, a steady and coherent evolution occurred in the Howard Government's depiction of the Australia-China relationship. It developed from an economic relationship (1996), to an economic relationship with strategic significance (1997), to a strategic economic relationship (2003), and finally to an explicit strategic relationship (2004). These positive depictions were compelled by insecurity rather than a genuine strategic reorientation towards China. An overall assessment indicates that Australia was, in reality, strategically anxious regarding China, and only depicted itself as growing close to China. A quick summary of key statements across the Howard years clearly displays some of the evidence for this strategic anxiety. During the 1996 Taiwan Strait crisis, Downer responded to the US deployment of two aircraft carrier groups by saying that it was 'a very clear demonstration by the United States that it is interested in maintaining its involvement in the security of the region and we obviously welcome that'.[7] The 1997 Department of Foreign Affairs and Trade White Paper, *In the National Interest*, stated that:

> Within East Asia, US strategic engagement in the region is widely regarded as a crucial stabilising influence, and an indispensable condition for the continuing strategic stability on which the region's economic success is ultimately dependent. Without it, regional countries might seek to significantly expand their defence capability in a destabilising way.[8]

In 1999 Downer said 'we should not succumb to any false notions that we have some kind of 'special' relationship with China',[9] and in 2000 Howard said 'we do have a high technology Defence Force as far as Taiwan is concerned'.[10] During the 2001 Australia–China Taiwan Strait incident, Howard said 'China's always had a different view about what international law allows the vessels of one country to do in the territorial waters of another. There's nothing new about that'.[11] The 2003 *Defence Update* announced that 'strategic competition between the [United States] and China [would] continue over the next decade, and [that] the possibility of miscalculation over Taiwan persists'.[12] In 2005 Howard said that 'no relationship of substance in Asia has been more important over the years for Australia than our relationship with Japan'.[13] And, finally, the 2005 *Defence Update* observed that 'the pace and scale of China's defence modernisation may create the potential for misunderstandings, particularly with the development of new military strike capabilities that extend the strike capability and sustainability of its forces'.[14]

Thus a key question emerging from this investigation's findings is, why was Australia depicting itself as growing close to China when it was anxious about China's rise? A number of strategies, seven to be exact, can be hypothesised.

First, Australia may have depicted itself as drawing close to China to alert and shock the United States about growing regional trends; China's diplomacy with the Association of Southeast Asian Nations has been successful in recent times. This would compel the United States to work harder at maintaining its alliance with Australia, and provide it with an incentive to build up its other security alliances in the region, especially those with Japan and South Korea. The ideal result would be closer US-Australia relations because of increased US efforts to court Australia, and greater US security interaction and relations with other states in the region.[15] This would be to Australia's advantage, reducing the security burden on Australia for supporting the United States in the region. In addition, it may have been to compel the United States to increase its ANZUS commitment, placing fewer burdens upon Australia's self-reliance defence posture. If the United States was to build up its regional alliances, Australia's support in a Taiwan contingency would become less important. Hence the complexity of such a strategy is that, while Australia actually feared China, it depicted itself as drawing closer to China in an effort to compel its other security partners to work harder at containing China. This touches a traditional theme within international relations between entrapment and abandonment between senior and junior alliance partners.[16] Hence the depiction is one of Australia growing closer to China, while Australia's collective actions with its other security partners indicated that Australia was subtly hedging against China.[17] But a negative outcome of such a depiction strategy is that China may have become more insecure and adversarial as a result of it perceiving increased containment activity by countries such as the United States and Japan.

Second, Australia may have depicted itself as drawing closer to China so as to make China feel less insecure. If China was to see itself as increasingly engaged and integrated into the Asia-Pacific community, and its 'peaceful development' diplomacy as successful, it may have assumed a more relaxed view of regional security arrangements, and pursued foreign policy interests in a benign fashion.[18] Australia may have mistrusted China as a responsible regional actor, but the best policy to dampen China's insecurities was to become friendlier toward it. As a result, Australia's security position was more secure because China felt safer.

Third, Australia depicting itself as drawing closer to China may have been driven by domestic political incentives. The Howard Government may have emphasised good relations as an attack against Labor, which had previously castigated Howard's engagement (or lack thereof) with regard to Asia. Prior to the Howard Government's election in 1996, Labor Prime Minister Paul Keating predicted that Asian governments would reject Howard, whose populist support for Australian values and ANZUS had left him vulnerable to domestic political attack. These accusations by Keating and 'The Establishment' seemed to become a common critique of the Howard Government, accentuated by Howard's close ties to US President George W. Bush.[19] As Paul Kelly has noted, 'The Establishment' exercises considerable influence over foreign policy debate in Australia, and negating its influence was a key goal of the Howard Government towards protecting its public image. Depicting strong relations with China alongside a reinvigorated ANZUS to some extent shut down an avenue of criticism previously employed by the Opposition party and destabilised the consensus within 'The Establishment' on how Australian foreign policy should be conducted.[20]

Fourth, Australia may have been genuinely drawing closer to China (rather than a mere depiction) because the Howard Government judged that economic interests are Australia's most important foreign policy interest. This may have been motivated by the fear that China, as Australia's largest trade partner, could hurt and punish Australia economically. In accordance with this rationale, economic security is Australia's key interest, resulting in a corresponding alignment with China in strategic interests. Because China is powerful, it can dictate a holistic, comprehensive program of engagement with Australia that is not limited to economic interaction. However, this argument is limited by factual evidence. Although Australia has a strategic dialogue and defence exchange program with China, corresponding strategic alignment of a substantive nature has not been evident. Instead, the Howard Government's strategic actions exhibited a developing alignment with Japan.

Fifth, Australia may genuinely view China as a rising military power that will compete with and eventually surpass the United States in the future. Therefore, it is prudent for Australia to draw closer to China while it is still relatively weak, winning its confidence and trust. In essence, this strategy views China as Australia's best future security and strategic partner outright, rather than the United States. Downer's 2004 announcement of a 'strategic relationship' with China and revisionist interpretation of ANZUS could therefore have been a portent of future changes. This view would see China, as an Asian power, more capable of providing security, both economic and military, to Australia, than the United States, which is a Pacific power. However, this argument is again highly speculative. China's defence modernisation program is presently catered towards a Taiwan contingency rather than challenging the broader regional maritime dominance of the United States, and the US defence budget continues to outspend the Chinese defence budget by a considerable margin.[21]

Sixth, drawing closer to China may be part of a genuine grand strategic scheme of engagement and integration into Asia. Confirming Downer's 1996 declaration that 'engagement with Asia is our highest foreign policy priority', becoming close to China would be one important aspect of Australia drawing close to Asia in general.[22] Australia's signing of the Association of Southeast Asian Nation's Treaty of Amity and Cooperation in December 2005 and consequent entry into the East Asia Summit could be read as indicative of a broader regional strategy to become more closely integrated into Asia's economic and security forums. The question, therefore, is not so much is Australia's foreign policy becoming Sinofied, but Asianised?

Seventh, the Howard Government may not have had any strategy of positive depictions of China. In essence, it is an ad hoc policy, subject to the winds of political fortune. When trade is strong, Australia-China relations are strong; when trade is weak, Australia-China relations are weak. Even when diplomatic relations are poor, as in 1996, the government can still positively depict China because trade relations are relatively stable. According to this argument, the Howard Government's depiction of China was solely dependent on the health of the trade relationship. While the other six arguments show an active Howard Government conscious of its ability to shape its relationship with China through policy depictions, this option sees the government as ambivalent to the events and trends in the relationship and the broader Asia-Pacific region.

Although each of the seven hypotheses exhibits a degree of merit, the first three represent the most plausible arguments for the Howard Government's overarching strategy throughout its time in power. Positive depictions sought to compel the United States to work harder in the region, allay Chinese fears of containment, and shut down an avenue of domestic criticism towards Howard Government foreign policy. The reasonableness of these three strategies was based primarily upon the government's underlying concerns regarding China's rise which were exhibited in cautionary depictions of China. The occasional cautionary depictions of China highlighted an outstanding characteristic of this investigation: the Howard Government's tightly managed depiction of China. The government was pleased to announce the signing of new trade agreements with China and to promote the growing trade relationship. But the government typically abstained from commenting negatively on China's military modernisation program and growing strategic weight.

The Howard Government's cautionary statements concerning China's rise were very carefully constructed and sparingly distributed. That the Howard Government consistently produced essentially vacuous, ambiguous statements regarding China could be read as a sign of strategic unease. As Robert Jervis noted, 'actors do not pay careful attention to the images they have of other states—or the images they project—in periods when they believe everyone has the same goals and view of the world'.[23]

Australia's careful and considered statements about China are arguably key indicators that doubt pervaded the Howard Government's perceptions about China's rise. Despite speculations about the Australian Government's Sinofication of its strategic interests, in reality the government's behaviour revealed a constant angst about China. This angst was not a new phenomenon in Australia's perception of China. Neither were positive depictions. As Lachlan Strahan has noted, historically 'China's potent presence engendered various Australian responses, ranging from antagonism through accommodation to celebration'.[24] Why do these contradicting images of China persist in Australian public discourse and policy depictions? As Strahan notes, China often represents the mythological *El Dorado* come true in Australian capitalism, and an ominous and alien political culture at the same time. Ever since China began opening its markets in the 1970s, Australia's resource export industries have prospered.[25] Yet there is a profound sense of distrust within Australian policy towards China, in response to what Strahan has described as 'the third loss of China'.[26] According to Strahan:

> This time China fell not to Communism, nor to anti-Soviet ultra radicalism, but to 'market socialism', to the partial reintroduction of 'bourgeois' private enterprise. Many on the Australian Left were bewildered or angered by the growth of so-called 'Red Millionaires' in the latest incarnation of the New China.[27]

Here lies the evasive truth about Australian angst towards China. While policy has continually praised the benefits of the 'Chinese El Dorado', at the same time it has been frightened by an authoritarian system that survived the Cold War. The government that thwarted the Tiananmen Square uprising also escalated tensions in the 1996 Taiwan Strait crisis, played 'chicken' with an

American EP-3 spy plane in 2001, and has annual double digit defence budget growth.[28]

At a glance, Australia's new best friend is an authoritarian, market socialist regime that has survived the Cold War stronger, more powerful, and versatile to shift with and to shape its strategic environs. In essence, the Chinese system is a model that threatens the nature of democracy held dear by Australia. China is not just alien to Australia ethnically—its political culture and religious values embodied in the state cannot be reconciled to the Australian image of freedom and political felicity. In a poignant symbol, Strahan has identified the traditional Chinese symbol—the dragon—as a double-edged sword in relation to Australian perceptions of China. Strahan concludes: 'The dragon image, as I have argued, has always had benign and malevolent meanings. A dragon may bestow good fortune or it may swallow its prey.'[29]

Hence, the predominantly positive depiction of China that the Howard Government produced was a strategic decision, keeping strategic anxiety out of public discourse. The occasional Howard Government statements of strategic caution served to remind us that China is a sensitive and reflective strategic force on the rise. Economic expansion with China was an easy story to sell for the Howard Government because, first, it was based upon a buoyant long-term trade relationship that began bearing fruit after the Second World War; and second, the Australian public was willing to invest in the trade policy, benefiting both from employment opportunities and tax cuts. The Australian economy recorded its fifteenth year of continual growth in 2007.[30] It appears that, as Australia prospers as a result of the export driven 'resources boom', public perceptions of China continue to soften.[31] But how to present China's strategic and military rise has been a far more sensitive issue, both in presentation to the Australian polity and Australia's observant neighbours, in particular China and the United States.

The issue that emerges from the Howard years is not whether Australia-China relations were strong; at face value, they evidently were. The question is whether predominantly depicting China positively and as having a strategic relationship with Australia constitutes good policy (since Australia harbours real concerns about China's rise, as this investigation has shown). Consider Japan as a case study for comparative policy depictions analysis. Japan-China economic relations are very positive (like Australia). However, Japan-China political relations are very poor (unlike Australia). The Japan-China relationship has been described as 'cold politics, hot economy'.[32] Does this policy of adversarial relations and depictions achieve Japan's strategic interests? Obviously Japan's immediate strategic neighbourhood is markedly different to that of Australia, but the fact that it can conduct poor diplomatic relations while maintaining a buoyant trade relationship with China reveals that other policy depiction alternatives are available to Australia.

A subsidiary question, therefore, is what did a general depiction of China as a friend convey about the Howard Government's strategic goals of such depictions—which nevertheless, on occasion, reverted to revealing the Howard Government's true feeling of strategic unease towards China? At the outset, this investigation cited Jervis, who noted that 'a desired image can often be of greater use than a significant increment of military or economic power'.[33] For Australia, maintaining a positive image of China in government depictions, as part of a broader hedging strategy, was a relatively cheap policy alternative to other options for addressing China's rise.[34]

Conclusively then, the Howard Government's strategic *depiction* of China was construed as one of economic *and* strategic alignment and integration. It steadily evolved from one of economic alignment during the 1997–2002 period to one of strategic alignment and integration during 2003–2006. However, the Howard Government's strategic *perception* of China was persistently one of distrust, anxiety and unease. When the Labor Government of Prime Minister Kevin Rudd took office in December 2007, it was likely that this enduring historical dimension of Australia's view towards China would continue into the future.

Recent events lend support to the argument that the Howard Government's positive depiction of China was a result of insecurity rather than a bona fide strategic alignment. The developing Trilateral Security Dialogue between Australia, Japan and the United States provides a firm piece of supporting evidence to the case that Australia is conducting a hedging strategy in the region rather than a more revolutionary shift to China's sphere of influence in a regional balance of power system.[35] The 2007 *Defence Update* stated that 'Australia has no closer nor more valuable partner in the region than Japan'.[36] It goes on to say that 'Japan has made valuable contributions to operations in East Timor and Iraq, and Australia welcomes its efforts to contribute more directly to regional and global security'.[37] If the Howard Government had genuinely reoriented itself towards China, building security relations with Japan would have been a strategic error. In such circumstances, the Howard Government's 2007 Australia–Japan Joint Declaration on Security Cooperation could have been a mistake.[38] It would have allowed the emergence of a second strategic conundrum synonymous to Australia's current predicament with the US–Australia–China triangle. Australia might have been forced to choose between good relations with either Japan or China, if tensions had arisen.

In truth, the Howard Government's move towards China was more image than reality. For Australia, hedging was a sensible approach, investing in its existing security relationships, while inviting China into the regional security architecture. If attempts to integrate China had failed, Australia would have still possessed strong alliances in the region to balance with against China. By investing in security ties with Japan, the Howard Government attempted to strengthen a weaker link in the regional US alliance network. Even so, today China remains ultimately responsible as to whether it will adhere to the existing US-led system, and consequently maintain close relations with Australia, or whether it will forcibly revise the existing order, which would force Australia to distance itself from China, and support the United States and Japan more. As Hugh White has noted, China is facing an important decision. For the United States to accept China's emerging leadership role in the region (ideally in a power-sharing arrangement), China will have to accept that Japan also has a legitimate leadership role to play in the region.[39] In lieu of this fact, the Howard Government's dual engagement of Japan and China sets an important integrating precedent for stable Asia-Pacific relations in the future. If China continues a peaceful foreign policy consistent with the past 30 years, Australia may be compelled in the distant future, as may the United States, to considerably revise its perceptions about Chinese power as a proven 'peaceful development'.[40] Until such a day arrives, judging the success of 'Howard's Long March' will remain a difficult task.

ENDNOTES

[1] The report suggests that the United States should cultivate an economic relationship with Australia of strategic significance, equivalent to the current Chinese economic relationship with Australia. See 'China's Military Modernization and Cross-Strait Balance', hearing before the US–China Economic and Security Review Commission, One Hundred Ninth Congress, First Session, 15 September 2005, p. 232.

[2] Alexander Downer, address to the International Institute for Strategic Studies/Strategic and Defence Studies Centre Conference, 'The New Security Agenda in the Asia Pacific Region', available at <http://www.dfat.gov.au/media/speeches/foreign/1996/regsec5.html>, accessed 3 April 2007.

[3] Michael Wesley, *The Howard Paradox: Australian Diplomacy in Asia from 1996-2006*, ABC Books, Sydney, 2007, p. 218.

[4] Alexander Downer, 'Media Conference:17 August 2004', Beijing, available at <http://www.foreignminister.gov.au/transcripts/2004/040817_ds_beijing.html>, accessed 2 April 2007.

[5] Hugh White said on the affair: 'My take is that Downer was in the wrong place, at the wrong time and in the wrong way delivered a message it was important to deliver.' White also said: 'You never want to do it in Beijing, because the Chinese will interpret it as a result of their pressure, the Americans will too, and it's undignified. You don't do it in a doorstop, but rather in a considered, formal statement of policy. And you don't do it sideways by talking about ANZUS.' See Greg Sheridan, 'Taiwan gaffe puts delicate balance at risk', *Australian*, 21 August 2004, p. 31.

[6] Downer, 'Media Conference', 17 August 2004.

[7] Don Greenlees and Richard McGregor, 'Downer warns China over war games', *Australian*, 13 March 1996, p. 8.

[8] Department of Foreign Affairs and Trade, *In the National Interest*, Commonwealth of Australia, Canberra, 1997, p. 29.

[9] Alexander Downer, 'Australia and China—Partners for Progress', address at the 1999 China Oration of the Australia–China Business Council, Sydney, 25 November 1999, available at <http://www.dfat.gov.au/media/speeches/foreign/1999/991125_aust_china.html>, accessed 10 April 2007.

[10] John Howard, 'Interview with Steve Liebmann', 5 May 2000, available at <http://www.pm.gov.au/media/interview/2000/today0505.cfm>, accessed 1 April 2007.

[11] John Howard, 'Interview with Tracy Grimshaw', 30 April 2001, available at <http://www.pm.gov.au/media/interview/2001/interview994.cfm>, accessed 5 March 2007.

[12] Department of Defence, *Australia's National Security: A Defence Update 2003*, Commonwealth of Australia, Canberra, p. 8.

[13] John Howard, 'Australian Outlook: Australian Policy Priorities for the Asia Pacific', address to the Asia Society, New York, 12 September 2005, available at <http://www.asiasociety.org.au/speeches/speeches_current/s42_John_Howard_NY.htm>, accessed 28 November 2008.

[14] Department of Defence, *Australia's National Security: A Defence Update 2005*, Commonwealth of Australia, Canberra, 2005, available at <http://www.defence.gov.au/update2005/defence_update_2005.pdf>, accessed 28 November 2008, p. 6.

[15] 'China's Military Modernization and Cross-Strait Balance', hearing before the US–China Economic and Security Review Commission, One Hundred Ninth Congress, First Session, 15 September 2005, p. 232.

[16] Victor D. Cha, *Alignment Despite Antagonism: The US-Korea-Japan Security Triangle*, Stanford University Press, Stanford, 1999, p. 37.

[17] Hedging in this scenario can be described informally as 'buying insurance'. As Medeiros argues, hedging constitutes a 'geopolitical insurance strategy' that combines engagement, binding and balancing into an overall policy position that 'possesses both cooperative and competitive dimension'. See Evan S. Medeiros, 'Strategic Hedging and the Future of Asia-Pacific Stability', *The Washington Quarterly*, vol. 29, no. 1 (Winter 2005–06), pp. 145–67 at pp. 147–48.

[18] 'Peaceful development' has become the preferred phrase within Chinese foreign policy to describe China's rise, rather than the more disputable 'peaceful rise' term. See *People's Daily Online*, available at <http://english.people.com.cn/zhuanti/Zhuanti_458.html>, accessed 28 November 2008.

[19] Paul Kelly describes 'The Establishment' as 'a loose identity among the retired public servants, retired senior military officers, intellectuals, academics, economists, and journalists involved in the international policy debate'. See Paul Kelly, *Howard's decade: An Australian Foreign Policy Reappraisal*, Lowy Institute Paper no. 15, Lowy Institute for International Policy, Sydney, 2006. p. 6.

[20] Kelly, *Howard's decade: An Australian Foreign Policy Reappraisal*, p. 7.

[21] According to *The Military Balance*, the US defence budget for 2006 was US$559 billion, compared to US$35.3 billion for China. Even when considering the Chinese Government significantly under-reports its military expenditure, these figures still represent a significant disparity in economic resources. See *The Military Balance 2007* (for The International Institute for Strategic Studies), Routledge, London, p. 28 (figures for the United States), and p. 346 (figures for China).

[22] Alexander Downer, address to the Foreign Correspondents' Association, Sydney, 11 April 1996, available at <http://www.dfat.gov.au/media/speeches/foreign/1996/asia-long.html>, accessed 8 March /2007.

[23] Robert Jervis, *The Logic of Images in International Relations*, Princeton University Press, Princeton, 1970, p. 13.

[24] Lachlan Strahan, *Australia's China: Changing perceptions from the 1930s to the 1990s*, Cambridge University Press, Cambridge, 1996, p. 289.

[25] See Strahan, *Australia's China: Changing perceptions from the 1930s to the 1990s*, p. 298. Strahan noted that 'Australian exports to China climbed from $97 million in 1973 to $422 million in 1978, reaching a high-water mark of $1.587 billion in 1986'.

[26] Strahan, *Australia's China: Changing perceptions from the 1930s to the 1990s*, p. 311.

[27] Strahan, *Australia's China: Changing perceptions from the 1930s to the 1990s*, p. 311.

[28] Strahan, *Australia's China: Changing perceptions from the 1930s to the 1990s*, p. 314.

[29] Strahan, *Australia's China: Changing perceptions from the 1930s to the 1990s*, p. 315.

[30] Department of Foreign Affairs and Trade, *Trade 2006*, Commonwealth of Australia, Canberra, 2006, p. 11.

[31] The warmth Australians feel towards China is now comparative to the warm feelings it has towards the United States. In a 2006 Lowy Institute for International Policy poll, 62 per cent of respondents expressed warm feelings towards the United States, and 61 per cent expressed warm feelings towards China. See Ivan Cook, *The Lowy Institute Poll 2006: Australia, Indonesia and the world: Public Opinion*

and Foreign Policy, Lowy Institute for International Policy, Sydney, 2006, available at <http://www.lowyinstitute.org/Publication.asp?pid=470>, accessed 28 November 2008, p. 6.

[32] Tomohiko Taniguchi, 'A Cold Peace: The Changing Security Equation in Northeast Asia', *Orbis*, vol. 49, no. 3, Summer 2005, p. 445.

[33] Jervis, *The Logic of Images in International Relations*, p. 6.

[34] For example, other policy options include an increased military budget, or improved economic competitiveness through lower tax rates, and corresponding reduction in social services, to allow increased defence spending.

[35] For an example of this developing trilateral security partnership, consider recent discussions of a trilateral missile defence system between the United States, Australia and Japan. See 'We will help with missile shield: Downer', *Australian*, 24 May 2007, available at <http://www.theaustralian.news.com.au/story/0,20867,21786413-31477,00.html>, accessed 25 May 2007.

[36] Department of Defence, *A Defence Update 2007: Protecting our People, Interests and Values*, Commonwealth of Australia, Canberra, 5 July 2007, available at <http://www.defence.gov.au/ans/2007/contents_pdf.htm>, accessed 28 November 2008, p. 19.

[37] Department of Defence, *A Defence Update 2007: Protecting our People, Interests and Values*, p. 19.

[38] Department of Foreign Affairs and Trade, 'Australia–Japan Joint Declaration on Security Cooperation', Tokyo, 13 March 2007, available at <http://www.dfat.gov.au/geo/japan/aus_jap_security_dec.html>, accessed 27 July 2007.

[39] Hugh White, 'The limits to optimism: Australia and the rise of China', *Australian Journal of International Affairs*, vol. 59, no. 4, December 2005, p. 478.

[40] *People's Daily Online*, available at <http://english.people.com.cn/zhuanti/Zhuanti_458.html>, accessed 28 November 2008.

Bibliography

Books and Book Chapters

Dalrymple, Rawdon, *Continental Drift: Australia's Search for a Regional Identity*, Ashgate Publishing Limited, Hampshire, 2003.

Gyngell, Allan and Michael Wesley, *Making Australian Foreign Policy*, Cambridge University Press, Port Melbourne, 2003.

Harris, Stuart, *Will China Divide Australia and the US?*, The Australian Centre for American Studies, Sydney, 1998.

Jervis, Robert, *The Logic of Images in International Relations*, Princeton University Press, Princeton, 1970.

Malik, Mohan, 'Australia and China: Divergence and Convergence of Interests', in James Cotton and John Ravenhill (eds), *The National Interest in a Global Era: Australia in Global Affairs 1996–2000*, Oxford University Press, Melbourne, 2002, pp. 109–129.

Sutter, Robert G., 'Appendix: Australian Perspectives on China's Approach to Asia and Implications for the United States', in Robert G. Sutter, *China's Rise in Asia: Promises and Perils*, Rowman and Littlefield Publishers, Lanham, 2005, pp. 281–87.

Wesley, Michael, *The Howard Paradox: Australian Diplomacy in Asia 1996–2006*, ABC Books, Sydney, 2007.

Zhang, Jian, 'Australia and China: Towards a Strategic Partnership?', in James Cotton and John Ravenhill (eds), *Trading on Alliance Security: Australia in World Affairs 2001–2005*, Oxford University Press, Melbourne, 2007, pp. 89–111.

Government Publications and Statements

(all sub-items of entries are in chronological order)

Department of Defence, *Australia's National Security: A Defence Update 2005*, Commonwealth of Australia, Canberra, 2005, available at <http://www.defence.gov.au/update2005/defence_update_2005.pdf>, accessed 26 February 2007.

————, *Australia's National Security: A Defence Update 2003*, Commonwealth of Australia, Canberra, 2003, available at <http://www.defence.gov.au/ans2003/Report.pdf>, accessed 26 February 2007.

————, *Defence 2000: Our Future Defence Force*, Commonwealth of Australia, Canberra, 2000, available at

<http://www.defence.gov.au/whitepaper/docs/WPAPER.PDF>, accessed 26 February 2007.

Department of Foreign Affairs and Trade, '2006 Australia-United States Ministerial Consultations Joint Communiqué', Washington, DC, 12 December 2006, available at <http://www.dfat.gov.au/geo/us/ausmin06_joint_communique.html>, accessed 6 April 2007.

———, *Advancing the National Interest: Australia's Foreign and Trade Policy White Paper*, Commonwealth of Australia, Canberra, 2003.

———, 'Taiwan Brief', October 1998, Commonwealth of Australia, Canberra, 1998, available at <http://www.dfat.gov.au/geo/tawan/taiwan.pdf>, accessed 4 March 2007.

———, 'Address to launch the EAAU [East Asian Analytical Unit] study "China Embraces the Market: Achievements, Constraints and Opportunities"', Sydney, 21 April 1997, available at <http://www.dfat.gov.au/media/speeches/foreign/1997/eaau.html>, accessed 3 April 2007.

———, *In the National Interest: Australia's Foreign and Trade Policy White Paper*, Commonwealth of Australia, Canberra, 1997.

Downer, Alexander, 'Doorstop Interview Trilateral Strategic Dialogue', Sydney, 18 March 2006, available at <http://www.foreignminister.gov.au/transcripts/2006/060318_ds-3lat.html>, accessed 6 May 2007.

——— 'Joint Statement Australia–Japan–United States', Sydney, 18 March 2006, available at <http://www.foreignminister.gov.au/releases/2006/joint_statement-aus-japan_usa_180306.html>, accessed 6 May 2007.

———, 'Biennial Sir Arthur Tange Lecture in Australian Diplomacy', Canberra, 8 August 2005, available at <http://www.foreignminister.gov.au/speeches/2005/050808_tange.html>, accessed 26 February 2007.

———, 'Media conference', Beijing, 17 August 2004, available at <http://www.foreignminister.gov.au/transcripts/2004/040817_ds_beijing.html>, accessed 2 April 2007.

———, 'Doorstop interview', St Regis Hotel, Beijing, 16 August 2004, available at <http://www.foreignminister.gov.au/transcripts/2004/040816_ds.html>, accessed 2 April 2007.

———, 'Australia and China's Shared Interests—Security and Strategic Dimensions', speech to the Australia–China Free Trade Agreement

Conference, Sydney, 13 August 2004, available at
<http://www.foreignminister.gov.au/speeches/2004/040813_aus_china_fta.html>,
accessed 2 April 2007.

————, 'Australia and China—Partners for Progress', speech at the 1999 China
Oration of the Australia–China Business Council, Sydney, 25 November
1999, available at <http://www.dfat.gov.au/media/speeches/foreign/
1999/991125_aust_china.html>, accessed 10 April 2007.

————, 'Release of James Peng', 14 November 1999, available at
<http://www.dfat.gov.au/media/releases/foreign/1999/fa129_99.html>,
accessed 16 March 2007.

————, 'NATO Bombing of Chinese Embassy', 10 May 1999, available at
<http://www.dfat.gov.au/media/releases/foreign/1999/fa047_99.html>,
accessed 16 March 2007.

————, 'Australia and Asia—After the Crisis', Occasional Lecture to the
Business/Academic Meeting of the Asia Research Centre and the WA
State Office of the Department of Foreign Affairs and Trade, Perth, 6
August 1998, available at
<http://www.dfat.gov.au/media/speeches/foreign/
1998/980806-asia-crsis.html>, accessed 3 April 2007.

————, 'China signs International Human Rights Covenant', 28 October 1997,
available at
<http://www.dfat.gov.au/media/releases/foreign/1997/fa131_97.html>,
accessed 10 April 2007.

————, 'Address to the 1997 Australia in Asia Series', Sydney, 10 September
1997, available at <http://www.dfat.gov.au/media/speeches/foreign/
1997/china10Sept97.html>, accessed 10 April 2007.

————, 'First Round of Human Rights Dialogue with China: $300,000 Cooperation
Program Launched', 14 August 1997, available at
<http://www.dfat.gov.au/media/releases/foreign/1997/fa95_97.html>,
accessed 10 April 2007.

————, 'Announcement of Bilateral Regional Security Dialogues', 28 July 1997,
available at <http://www.dfat.gov.au/media/releases/foreign/1997/
fa84_97.html>, accessed 10 April 2007.

————, 'China: Human Rights', 10 April 1997, available at
<http://www.dfat.gov.au/media/releases/foreign/1997/fa24_97.html>,
accessed 10 April 2007.

————, 'Address to the Australian College of Defence and Strategic Studies',
Canberra, 6 December 1996, available at

<http://www.dfat.gov.au/media/speeches/foreign/
1996/regional_coop_security.html>, accessed 2 April 2007.

———, 'Australia's place in the world', address to the NSW Division of the
Liberal Party, Sydney, 26 November 1996, available at
<http://www.dfat.gov.au/media/speeches/foreign/1996/1996/nsw-dii.html>,
accessed 3 April 2007.

———, 'Australia's Commitment to the Region', address to the Asia–Australia
Institute, University of New South Wales, Sydney, 6 November 1996,
available at <http://www.dfat.gov.au/media/speeches/foreign/
1996/asia_ins.html>, accessed 3 April 2007.

———, 'Australia and its Neighbours', 1 November 1996, available at
<http://parlinfoweb.aph.gov.au/piweb/view_document.aspx?ID=6636&TABLE=
PRESSREL>, accessed 6 April 2007.

———, 'Question on notice: Uranium Sales to Taiwan', 31 October 1996, available
at
<http://parlinfoweb.aph.gov.au/piweb/view_document.aspx?id=62018&
table=HANSARDR>, accessed 8 April 2007.

———, 'The Asia Pacific: gearing up for the twenty first century', address to
the Asia Society, New York, 27 September 1996, available at
<http://parlinfoweb.aph.gov.au/piweb/view_document.aspx?ID=12124&TABLE=
PRESSREL>, accessed 6 April 2007.

———, 'Australia and China agree on Australian Consulate General in Hong
Kong after July 1, 1997', 22 August 1996, available at
<http://parlinfoweb.aph.gov.au/piweb/view_document.aspx?ID=8898&TABLE=
PRESSREL>, accessed 6 April 2007.

———, 'Media release, Ministerial visit to China', 15 August 1996, available at
<http://www.dfat.gov.au/media/releases/foreign/1996/fa78.html>,
accessed 16 March 2007.

———, 'Australia-United States Ministerial Consultations: joint communiqué',
27 July 1996, available at
<http://parlinfoweb.aph.gov.au/piweb/view_document.aspx?ID=2144&TABLE=
PRESSREL>, accessed 6 April 2007.

———, 'Australia-United States: a strategic partnership for the twenty-first
century: Sydney Statement: joint security declaration', 27 July 1996,
available at
<http://parlinfoweb.aph.gov.au/piweb/view_document.aspx?ID=3379&TABLE=
PRESSREL>, accessed 6 April 2007.

———, 'Australia, North East Asia and China: Opportunities in a Changing
World', address at a joint Asia/Austcham luncheon, Hong Kong, 4 July

1996, available at <http://www.dfat.gov.au/media/speeches/foreign/ 1996/hongkong>, accessed 5 March 2007.

———, 'Question without Notice: DIFF Scheme', 18 June 1996, available at <http://parlinfoweb.aph.gov.au/piweb/view_document.aspx?id=48386&table= HANSARDR>, accessed 7 April 2007.

———, 'Media release: Chinese Nuclear Test', 8 June 1996, available at <http://www.dfat.gov.au/media/releases/foreign/1996/fa46.html>, accessed 16 March 2007.

———, 'Australia and Japan: cooperation in the region', statement at Japan's National Press Club, Tokyo, 6 June 1996, available at <http://parlinfoweb.aph.gov.au/piweb/view_document.aspx?ID=17796&TABLE= PRESSREL>, accessed 29 March 2007.

———, 'Australia and the United States: A Vital Friendship', speech to the Australian Centre for American Studies, Sydney, 29 May 1996, available at <http://www.dfat.gov.au/media/speeches/foreign/1996/ aust_uni.html>, accessed 3 April 2007.

———, 'Question without Notice: Visas: Mayor of Taipei City', 28 May 1996, available at <http://parlinfoweb.aph.gov.au/piweb/view_document.aspx?id=58186&table= HANSARDR>, accessed 7 April 2007.

———, 'Security through Cooperation', address to the IISS/SDSC Conference, 'The New Security Agenda in the Asia Pacific Region', Canberra, 2 May 1996, available at <http://www.dfat.gov.au/media/speeches/foreign/ 1996/regsec5.html>, accessed 3 April 2007.

———, 'Australia and Asia: Taking the Long View', address to the Foreign Correspondents Association, Sydney, 11 April 1996, available at <http://dfat.gov.au/media/speeches/foreign/1996/asia-long.html>, accessed 8 March 2007.

———, 'Taiwan Elections', 24 March 1996, available at <http://parlinfoweb.aph.gov.au/piweb/view_document.aspx?ID=7333&TABLE= PRESSREL>, accessed 6 April 2007.

Fischer, Tim, 'A Twenty Five year Partnership Between Australia and China', address to the Australia–China Forum, Beijing, 8 September 1997, available at <http://www.dfat.gov.au/media/speeches/trade/1997/ a-c_forum8sept97.html>, accessed 20 April 2007.

Frost, Frank, *The United States and China: Containment or Engagement?,* Current Issues Brief no. 5, 1996–97, Foreign Affairs, Defence and Trade Group, available at <http://www.aph.gov.au/library/pubs/cib/ 1996-97/97cib5.htm>, accessed 15 March 2007.

Hill, Robert, 'Speech to IISS Shangri-La Dialogue', Singapore, 5 June 2005, available at <http://www.iiss.org/conferences/the-shangri-la-dialogue/ shangri-la-dcialogue-2005/2005-speeches/fourth-plenary-session-the-hon-robert-hill.html>, accessed 7 May 2007.

———, 'Joint Press Conference with United States Secretary for Defense Donald Rumsfeld', Shangri-La Hotel, Singapore, 5 June 2005, available at <http://www.minister.defence.gov.au/HillTranscripttpl.cfm?CurrentId=4907>, accessed 7 May 2007.

———, 'Media Release: Defence Minister Visits Singapore and China', 4 June 2005, available at <http://www.minister.defence.gov.au/Hilltpl.cfm?CurrentId=4905>, accessed 6 May 2007.

———, 'Question without notice: Dalai Lama', 17 September 1996, available at <http://parlinfoweb.aph.gov.au/piweb/view_document.aspx?id=726070&table= HANSARDS>, accessed 8 April 2007.

Howard, John, 'Doorstop interview', Imperial Hotel, Tokyo, 11 March 2007, available at <http://www.pm.gov.au/media/Interview/2007/ Interview24195.cfm>, accessed 27 March 2007.

———, 'Address to Australia India Business Council Lunch', Wentworth Hotel, Sydney, 1 September 2006, available at <http://www.pm.gov.au/media/speech/20062112.cfm>, accessed 17 April 2007.

———, 'Interview with David Speers', Batam, Indonesia, 27 June 2006, available at <http://www.pm.gov.au/media/interview/2006/Interview1997.cfm>, accessed 5 March 2007.

———, 'Address to the Luncheon in honour of His Excellency Mr Wen Jiabao, Premier of the State Council People's Republic of China', Parliament House, Canberra, 3 April 2006, available at <http://www.pm.gov.au/media/speech/2006/speech1855.cfm>, accessed 28 February 2007.

———, 'Joint Press Conference with His Excellency Mr Wen Jiabao, Premier of the State Council, People's Republic of China', Parliament House, Canberra, 3 April 2006, available at <http://www.pm.gov.au/media/interview/2006/Interview1854.cfm>, accessed 28 February 2007.

———, 'Press conference', Grand Hotel, Busan, 17 November 2005, available at <http://www.pm.gov.au/media/interview/2005/Interview1685.cfm>, accessed 1 April 2007.

————, 'Australian Outlook: Australian Policy Priorities for the Asia Pacific', address to the Asia Society, New York, 12 September 2005, available at <http://www.asiasociety.org.au/speeches/speeches_current/s42_John_Howard_NY.htm>, accessed 26 February 2007.

————, 'Doorstep interview', The Lodge, Canberra, 14 August 2005, available at <http://www.pm.gov.au/media/interview/2005/Interview1501.cfm>, accessed 31 March 2007.

————, 'Joint Press Conference with the President of the United States of America George W. Bush', The White House, Washington, DC, 19 July 2005, available at <http://www.pm.gov.au/media/interview/2005/Interview1472.cfm>, accessed 28 February 2007.

————, 'Joint Press Conference with Secretary of Defense Donald Rumsfeld', The Pentagon, Washington, DC, 18 July 2005, available at <http://www.pm.gov.au/media/interview/2005/Interview1469.cfm>, accessed 5 March 2007.

————, 'Doorstop interview', The Willard Intercontinental Hotel, Washington, DC, 16 July 2005, available at <http://www.pm.gov.au/media/interview/2005/Interview1465.cfm>, accessed 1 April 2007.

————, 'Press conference', St Regis Hotel, Beijing, 19 April 2005, available at <http://www.pm.gov.au/media/interview/2005/Interview1336.cfm>, accessed 31 March 2007.

————, 'Australia in the World', address to the Lowy Institute for International Policy, Sydney, 31 March 2005, available at <http://www.lowyinstitute.org/Publication.asp?pid=396>, accessed 26 February 2007.

————, 'Interview with John Miller and Ross Davie', Radio 4BC, Brisbane, 15 March 2005, available at <http://www.pm.gov.au/media/interview/2005/Interview1273.cfm>, accessed 1 April 2007.

————, 'Joint Press Conference with the Rt. Hon. Helen Clark, Prime Minister of New Zealand', Parliament House, Wellington, 21 February 2005, available at <http://www.pm.gov.au/media/interview/2005/Interview1254.cfm>, accessed 1 April 2007.

————, 'Doorstop interview', Adelaide, 20 August 2004, available at <http://www.pm.gov.au/media/interview/2004/Interview1088.cfm>, accessed 1 April 2007.

———, 'Interview with Neil Mitchell', Radio 3AW, 20 August 2004, available at <http://www.pm.gov.au/media/interview/2004/Interviewe1086.cfm>, accessed 31 March 2007.

———, 'Address to the Asialink—ANU National Forum: Australia's Engagement with Asia: A New Paradigm', 13 August 2004, available at <http://www.pm.gov.au/media/speech/2004/speech1069.cfm>, accessed 5 March 2007.

———, 'Doorstop interview', Beijing, 18 August 2003, available at <http://www.pm.gov.au/media/interview/2003/Interview438.cfm>, accessed 31 March 2007.

———, 'Doorstop interview', Beijing, 17 August 2003, available at <http://www.pm.gov.au/media/interview/2003/Interview436.cfm>, accessed 1 April 2007.

———, 'Interview with David Speers', 13 August 2003, available at <http://www.pm.gov.au/media/interview/2003/Interview423.cfm>, accessed 5 March 2007.

———, 'Press conference', St Regis Hotel, Beijing, 22 May 2002, available at <http://www.pm.gov.au/media/interview/2002/interview1663.cfm>, accessed 31 March 2007.

———, 'Briefing for Chinese Media', Parliament House, Canberra, 16 May 2002, available at <http://www.pm.gov.au/media/interview/2002/interview1649.cfm>, accessed 28 February 2007.

———, 'Interview with Tracy Grimshaw', Today Show, 30 April 2001, available at <http://www.pm.gov.au/media/interview/2001/interview994.cfm>, accessed 5 March 2007.

———, 'Doorstop interview', The Lodge, Canberra, 27 April 2001, available at <http://www.pm.gov.au/media/interview/2001/interview979.cfm>, accessed 5 March 2007.

———, 'Interview with Catherine McGrath', AM Programme, 26 April 2001, available at <http://www.pm.gov.au/media/interview/2001/interview965.cfm>, accessed 5 March 2007.

———, 'Radio interview with Alan Jones', 2UE, 6 December 2000, available at <http://www.pm.gov.au/media/interview/2000/interview576.cfm>, accessed 1 April 2007.

———, 'Interview with Steve Liebmann', Today Show, Channel 9, 5 May 2000, available at

<http://www.pm.gov.au/media/interview/2000/today0505.cfm>,
accessed 1 April 2007.

———, 'How Financial Reform is Working for Australia', address to the Asia
Society, New York, 15 July 1999, available at
<http://www.asiasociety.org/speeches/pmhoward.html>, accessed 26
February 2007.

———, 'Joint Press Conference', Willard Inter-Continental Hotel, Washington,
DC, 12 July 1999, available at
<http://www.pm.gov.au/media/interview/1999/jointpress1207.cfm>,
accessed 31 March 2007.

———, 'Press conference', Akasaka State Guest House, Tokyo, 6 July 1999,
available at
<http://www.pm.gov.au/media/interview/1999/akasaka0607.cfm>,
accessed 31 March 2007.

———, 'Address at the reception to mark the 25th Anniversary of Diplomatic
Relations between Australia and China', Sheraton on the Park, Sydney,
17 December 1997, available at
<http://www.pm.gov.au/media/speech/1997/china.cfm>, accessed 17
April 2007.

———, 'Doorstop interview following the meeting with Chinese President', Mr
Jiang Zemin, 24 November 1996, available at
<http://parlinfoweb.aph.gov.au/piweb/view_document.aspx?ID=9420&TABLE=
PRESSREL>, accessed 7 April 2007.

Klintworth, Gary, *Crisis Management: China, Taiwan and the United States—the
1995-96 Crisis and its Aftermath*, Research Paper no. 14, 1996–97, Foreign
Affairs, Defence and Trade Group, available at
<http://www.aph.gov.au/LIBRARY/pubs/rp/1996-97/97rp14.htm>,
accessed 2 April 2007.

MacLachlan, Ian, 'Media release: Australia-China Defence Minister's Talks',
19 February 1998, available at
<http://www.minister.defence.gov.au/1998/02298.html>, accessed 6
May 2007.

———, 'Australia's Strategic Policy', 2 December 1997, available at
<http://www.defence.gov.au/minister/sr97/s971202.html>, accessed 3
April 2007.

———, 'Personal Explanations', 7 May 1996, available at
<http://parlinfoweb.aph.gov.au/piweb/view_document.aspx?id=37670&table=
HANSARDR>, accessed 29 March 2007.

Richardson, Dennis, 'Address at the Brooking Institution', Washington, DC, 24 January 2006, available at <http://www.austemb.org.whwh/SpeechEAsia.html>, accessed 6 May 2007.

Rudd, Kevin, 'It's time to build an Asia Pacific Community', Address to the Asia Society, AustralAsia Centre, Sydney, available at <http://www.pm.gov.au/media/Speech/2008/speech_0286.cfm>, accessed 17 June 2008.

Rumsfeld, Donald, 'Speech to IISS Shangri-La Dialogue', Singapore, 4 June 2005, available at <http://www.iiss.org/conferences/the-shangri-la-dialogue/shangri-la-dialogue-2005/2005-speeches/first-plenary-session-the-hon-donald-rumsfeld.html>, accessed 7 May 2007.

Senate Foreign Affairs, Defence and Trade Committee, 'Opportunities and challenges: Australia's relationship with China', Commonwealth of Australia, Canberra, 10 November 2005, available at <http://www.aph.gov.au/Senate/committee/fadt_ctte/china/report01/index.htm>, accessed 26 February 2007.

———, 'China's emergence: implications for Australia', Commonwealth of Australia, Canberra, March 2006, available at <http://www.aph.gov.au/SENATE/committee/fadt_ctte/china/report02/report.pdf>, accessed 1 March 2007.

Sherlock, Stephen, 'Australia's Relations with China: What's the Problem?', Current Issues Brief no. 23, 1996–97, Foreign Affairs, Defence and Trade Group, available at <http://www.aph.gov.au/library/pubs/CIB/1996-97/97cib23.htm>, accessed 4 April 2007.

United States-China Economic and Security Review Commission, Washington, January 2006, 'China's Military Modernization and Cross-Strait Balance', hearing before the U.S.-China Economic and Security Review Commission, One Hundred Ninth Congress, First Session, 15 September 2005, available at <http://www.uscc.gov/hearings/2005hearings/transcripts/Sept15/05_09_15_trans.pdf>, accessed 15 April 2007.

United States Department of State, 'Joint U.S.–Australia Press Conference', Sydney, 29 July 1996, available at <http://dosfan.lib.uic.edu/ERC/briefing/dossec/1996/9607/960727dossec.html>, accessed 5 April 2007.

Wesley, Michael, 'The Challenges of China: Australian Perceptions and Reactions', National Defense University Working Paper, National Defense University, and US Pacific Command, in *Asian Perspectives on the*

Challenges of China, Papers from the Asia-Pacific Symposium, 7 and 8 March 2000, National Defense University Press, Washington, DC, 2001.

Journal Articles

Bisley, Nick, 'Asia-Pacific regionalism and preferential trade agreements: the Australian case', *International Relations of the Asia-Pacific*, vol. 4, 2004, pp. 239–64.

Chunlai, Shi, 'For better Sino-Australian relations', *Australian Journal of International Affairs*, vol. 56, no. 3, 2002, pp. 337–46.

Cotton, James, 'The Near North, the East Asian hemisphere, the Asia-Pacific: seeking direction in Australian foreign policy', *Australian Journal of International Affairs*, vol. 58, no. 1, March 2004, pp. 143–55.

Downer, Alexander, 'Securing Australia's interests—Australian foreign policy priorities', *Australian Journal of International Affairs*, vol. 59, no. 1, March 2005, pp. 7–12.

Flitton, Daniel, 'Issues in Australian Foreign Policy', *Australian Journal of Politics and History*, vol. 50, no. 2, 2004, pp. 229–46.

———, 'Perspectives on Australian foreign policy, 2002', *Australian Journal of International Affairs*, vol. 57, no. 1, 2003, pp. 37–54.

Garnaut, Ross, 'The sustainability and some consequences of Chinese economic growth', *Australian Journal of International Affairs*, vol. 59, no. 4, December 2005, pp. 509–518.

Gurry, Meg, 'Perspectives on Australian foreign policy, 2000', *Australian Journal of International Affairs*, vol. 55, no. 1, 2001, pp. 7–20.

Harris, Stuart, 'China's regional policies: how much hegemony?', *Australian Journal of International Affairs*, vol. 59, no. 4, December 2005, pp. 481–92.

———, 'China–US Relations: A Difficult Balancing Act for Australia?', *Global Change, Peace & Security*, vol. 17, no. 3, 2005, pp. 227–38.

Hogue, Cavan, 'Perspectives on Australian foreign policy, 1999', *Australian Journal of International Affairs*, vol. 54, no. 2, 2000, pp. 141–50.

Kapisthalam, Kaushik, 'Australia and Asia's rise', *Australian Journal of International Affairs*, vol. 60, no. 3, September 2006, pp. 369–75.

Kelton, Maryanne, 'Perspectives on Australian foreign policy, 2005', *Australian Journal of International Affairs*, vol. 60, no. 2, June 2006, pp. 229–46.

Leaver, Richard, 'The meanings, origins and implications of "the Howard Doctrine"', *The Pacific Review*, vol. 14, no. 1, 2001, pp. 15–34.

Mackerras, Colin, 'Australia–China Relations at the End of the Twentieth Century', *Australian Journal of International Affairs*, vol. 54, no. 2, 2000, pp. 185–200.

McDonald, Matt, 'Perspectives on Australian foreign policy, 2004', *Australian Journal of International Affairs*, vol. 59, no. 3, June 2005, pp. 153–68.

O'Connor, Brendon, 'Perspectives on Australian foreign policy', *Australian Journal of International Affairs*, vol. 58, no. 2, June 2004, pp. 207–220.

Pan, Chengxin, 'Neoconservatism, US–China conflict, and Australia's "great and powerful friends" dilemma', *The Pacific Review*, vol. 19, no. 4, December 2006, pp. 429–48.

Qingguo, Jia, 'Peaceful development: China's policy of reassurance', *Australian Journal of International Affairs*, vol. 59, no. 4, December 2005, pp. 493–507.

Richardson, Michael, 'Australia–Southeast Asia relations and the East Asian Summit', *Australian Journal of International Affairs*, vol. 59, no. 3, September 2005, pp. 351–65.

Rosecrance, Richard, 'Australia, China and the US', *Australian Journal of International Affairs*, vol. 60, no. 3, September 2006, pp. 364–68.

Smith, Gary, 'Perspectives on Australian Foreign Policy 1998', *Australian Journal of International Affairs*, vol. 53, no. 2, 1999, pp. 193–201.

Sutter, Robert, 'Thirty years of Australia-China relations: an American perspective', *Australian Journal of International Affairs*, vol. 56, no. 3, 2002, pp. 347–60.

Tow, William T., 'Deputy sheriff or independent ally? Evolving Australian-American ties in an ambiguous world order', *The Pacific Review*, vol. 17, no. 2, June 2004, pp. 271–90.

———, 'Sino-American relations and the "Australian factor": inflated expectations or discriminate engagement?', *Australian Journal of International Affairs*, vol. 59, no. 4, December 2005, pp. 451–67.

Tow, William T. and Leisa Hay, 'Australia, the United States and a "China growing strong": managing conflict avoidance', *Australian Journal of International Affairs*, vol. 55, no. 1, 2001, pp. 37–54.

Verrier, June R., 'Australia's self-image as a regional and international security actor: some implications of the Iraq war', *Australian Journal of International Affairs*, vol. 57, no. 3, November 2003, pp. 455–71.

Wesley, Michael, 'Perspectives on Australian foreign policy, 2001', *Australian Journal of International Affairs*, vol. 56, no. 1, 2002, pp. 47–63.

White, Hugh, 'The limits to optimism: Australia and the rise of China', *Australian Journal of International Affairs*, vol. 59, no. 4, December 2005, pp. 469–80.

Whitlam, Gough, 'Sino-Australian diplomatic relations 1972–2002', *Australian Journal of International Affairs*, vol. 56, no. 3, 2002, pp. 323–36.

Print Media and Think-Tanks

(all sub-items of entries are in chronological order)

AAP, 'US and China can work together, PM says', *Sydney Morning Herald*, 24 February 2007, available at <http://www.smh.com.au/news/NATIONAL/US-and-China-can-work-together-PM-says/2007/02/24/1171734066809.html>, accessed 28 February 2007.

Cook, Ivan, *The Lowy Institute Poll 2006: Australia, Indonesia and the world: Public Opinion and Foreign Policy*, Lowy Institute for International Policy, Sydney, 2006, available at <http://www.lowyinstitute.org/Publication.asp?pid=470>, accessed 26 May 2007.

Dibb, Paul, 'No reason to live in climate of fear', *Australian*, 6 February 2007, available at <http://www.theaustralian.news.com/au/story/0,20867,21175353-7583,00.html>, accessed 15 April 2007.

Dwyer, Michael and Louise Dodson, 'PM questions Howard's pull in Asia region', *Australian Financial Review*, 2 February 1996.

Dupont, Alan, 'Not the time to deal out Beijing', *Australian*, 26 March 2007, available at <http://www.theaustralian.news.com.au/printpage/0,5942,21444271,00.html>, accessed 15 April 2007.

Greenless, Don, and Richard McGregor, 'Downer warns China over war games', *Australian*, 13 March 1996.

Gyngell, Allan, 'There's rhetoric and dinner talk, but little debate on foreign policy', *Sydney Morning Herald*, 25 August 2003, available at <http://www.smh.com.au/articles/2003/08/24/1061663672744.html?from=storyrhs>, accessed 7 March 2007.

Hale, David D., *In the Balance: China's unprecedented growth and implications for the Asia-Pacific*, Australian Strategic Policy Institute, Canberra, February 2006.

Jennings, Peter, *Getting China Right: Australia's policy options for dealing with China*, Australian Strategic Policy Institute, Canberra, October 2005.

Jones, Tony, 'US watching Australia-China relations', *Lateline*, ABC, 22 June 2005, available at <http://www.abc.net.au/lateline/content/2005/s1398446.html>, accessed 6 March 2007.

Kelly, Paul, 'Security accord flags new Japan', *Australian*, 13 March 2007, available at <http://blogs.theaustralian.news.com.au/paulkelly/index.php/theaustralian/comments/security_accord_flags_new_japan.html>, accessed 15 April 2007.

———, *Howard's Decade: An Australian Foreign Policy Reappraisal,* Lowy Institute Paper no. 15, Lowy Institute for International Policy, Sydney, 2006.

Kelly, Paul and Richard McGregor, 'US ties no issue for China', *Australian*, 2 April 1997.

Malik, Mohan, 'The China Factor in Australia–U.S. Relations', *China Brief*, vol. 5, no. 8, The Jamestown Foundation, available at <http://www.jamestown.org/publications_details.php?volume_id=408&issue_id=3298&article_id=2369588.html>, accessed 2 April 2007.

McGregor, Richard, 'PM seeks strategic trade partnership', *Australian,* 1 April 1997.

Sheehan, Paul, 'Look east for the new reality show', *Sydney Morning Herald*, 21 January 2007, available at <http://www.smh.com.au/news/paul-sheehan?look-east-for-the-new-reality-show/2007/01/21/1169330763566.html>, accessed 28 February 2007.

———, 'The myth of one China – Taiwan: Special Report', *Australian*, 10 October 2006.

Sheridan, Greg, 'China lobby keeps India on the outer', *Australian*, 17 March 2007, available at <http://www.theaustralian.news.com.au/story/0,20867,21395372-25377,00.html>, accessed 15 April 2007.

———, 'Taiwan gaffe puts delicate balance at risk', *Australian*, 21 August 2004.

Stewart, Cameron, 'Spy drive to tackle Chinese', *Australian*, 28 December 2006, available at <http://www.theaustralian.news.com.au/story/0,20867,20980589-2702,00.html>, accessed 4 April 2007.

Symons, Emma-Kate and Joseph Kerr, 'PM eyes regional trade pact', *Australian*, 16 January 2007, available at <http://theaustralian.news.com.au/story/0,20867,21065497-601,00.html?from=public_rss>, accessed 1 March 2007.

Taylor, Nicholas, 'China as a Status Quo or Revisionist Power? Implications for Australia', *Security Challenges* (Kokoda Foundation), vol. 3, no. 1, February 2007.

Terril, Ross, *Riding the Wave: The rise of China and options for Australian policy*, Australian Strategic Policy Institute, Canberra, March 2006.

Thirwell, Mark, *The high price of feeding the hungry dragon*, Lowy Institute for International Policy, Sydney, 27 April 2006, available at <http://www.lowyinstitute.org/Publication.asp?pid=376>, accessed 2 March 2007.

Uren, David, 'China emerges as our biggest trade partner', *Australian*, 5 May 2007, available at <http://www.theaustralian.news.com.au/printpage/0,5942,21674786,00.html>, accessed 8 May 2007.

White, Hugh, 'Just who's afraid of China?', *Age*, 21 June 2006, available at <http://www.theage.com.au/news/opinion/just-whos-afraid-of-china/2006/06/20/1150701550076.html>, accessed 4 April 2007.

———, 'A rising China tests Australia's ties', *Age*, 18 March 2006, <http://www.theage.com.au/news/opinion/a-rising-china-tests-australias-ties/2006/03/17/1142582519984>, accessed 6 May 2007.

———, 'Handling China delicately', *Age*, 18 August 2005, available at <http://www.theage.com.au/news/hugh-white/handling-china-delicately/2005/08/17/1123958129532.html>, accessed 11 May 2007.

———, 'Things to chew over for the meat in the sandwich', *Sydney Morning Herald*, 18 August 2005, available at <http://www.smhcom.au/news/opinion/things-to-chew-over-for-the-meat-in-the-sandwich/2005/08/17/1123958125237.html>, accessed 8 April 2007.

———, 'Howard's Asian balancing act', *Age*, 13 April 2005, available at <http://www.theage.com.au/news/hugh-white/howards-asian-balancing-act/2005/04/12/1113251624114.html>, accessed 28 February 2007.

———, 'After Britain and then the US, China is in line to be our new best friend', *Sydney Morning Herald*, 24 March 2005, available at <http://www.smh.com.au/news/hugh-white/after-britain-and-then-the-us-china-is-in-line-to-be-our-new-best-friend/2005/03/23/1111525218301.html>, accessed 2 April 2007.

———, *The US, Taiwan and the PRC: Managing China's Rise: Policy Options for Australia*, Melbourne Asia Policy Papers, no. 5, Melbourne, November 2004.

Index

air combat capabilities 25
aircraft:
    Chinese J-8 fighter jet 24
    US EP-3 aircraft crisis 24, 52–3
alliances 25, 34–5, 37, 39, 49, 55
    ANZUS alliance 2, 5, 8, 11, 13, 35,
    37–8, 42, 49–51, 55n5 (*see also*
    treaties: ANZUS Treaty)
Anderson, John 12
Asia-Pacific Cities Summit 11
Asia-Pacific region 1–2, 4–5, 11, 19, 22,
    25, 32, 34–5, 39–40, 42, 50–1, 55
Asia-Pacific security architecture 5, 39–40
Association of Southeast Asian Nations
    (ASEAN) 4, 49
Australia (cities):
    Brisbane 11, 14n1
    Canberra 41
    Sydney 11, 43n40
Australia-China relations 1–5, 7–8, 10–14,
    14n1, 17–19, 21–2, 24–6, 27n7, 31,
    34–7, 39, 41–2, 47–8, 51, 53
Australia-Japan Joint Declaration on
    Security Cooperation (2007) 54
Australia-United States Ministerial
    Consultations (AUSMIN) 11, 14n1
    'Sydney Declaration' 11, 13
Australia-US relations 1, 35, 37–8, 49
Australia-US-China relations 1, 38, 54
Australian Defence Force (ADF) 1, 23–5,
    47, 49
Australian Government, AusAID 40
    2006 White Paper *Promoting Growth*
    and Stability 39
    aid programs 39–40
Australian Government, Department of
    Defence 11, 14, 20–1, 23, 25–6, 36,
    41, 45n68
    1997 Strategic Review *Australia's*
    Strategic Policy 20–2, 26, 41, 47
    2000 Defence White Paper *Defence*
    2000 25, 36, 43n33, 47
    2005 *Defence Update* 39, 41, 49
    2007 *Defence Update* 54

Australian Government, Department of
    Foreign Affairs and Trade (DFAT) 1,
    14n1, 20–1, 26, 31
    1997 DFAT White Paper *In the*
    National Interest 19–22, 26, 48
    2003 DFAT White Paper *Advancing*
    the National Interest 1, 4, 22,
    31–2, 41, 42n4
    Trade 2006 45n69
Australia-Japan Joint Declaration on
    Security Cooperation 54

behaviour 2–5, 9–10, 14, 23, 25, 33–4, 37,
    40–2, 52
bilateralism 8–11, 18–19, 26, 28n49,
    32–4, 39, 47
Blair, Dennis 33–4
Bush, George W. 36–8, 42, 50

Chen Shui-ban 11, 23
Chen Yonglin 37, 43n40
China:
    as a responsible regional actor 50, 55
    as a rising power 2, 5, 6n6, 8–9,
    14, 19–21, 26, 39–40, 47, 49, 52–5,
    56n18
    Beijing 11, 13, 17, 26, 27n7, 34, 38,
    42, 48, 55n5
    bombing of Chinese Embassy in
    Belgrade (9 May 1999) 22
    China's regional image 40
    dragon image in 53
    Hainan island 24
    Hong Kong special administrative
    region of 19
    Macau special administrative region
    of 22
    nuclear test (8 June 1996) by 9, 12–
    14, 14n1
    'one-China' policy 8, 19–20
    'peaceful development' of 2, 5, 6n6,
    22, 39–40, 50, 55, 56n18
    People's Liberation Army (PLA) 23,
    27n7
    People's Liberation Army Navy
    (PLAN) 45n68

power projection capabilities of 20,
25–6, 41
Qingdao province and port in 45n68
Shenzhen province in 11
Tiananmen Square incident in 10, 52
Tibet autonomous province in 12
Cold War 52–3
communications 3–4, 12, 14, 19, 26, 33,
37, 52–3
Comprehensive Test Ban Treaty (*see*
treaties: Comprehensive Test Ban
Treaty)
containment strategy 2, 11, 13–14, 14n1,
50–1
cooperation 5, 23, 26, 32–3, 40 (*see also*
Australia-Japan Joint Declaration on
Security Cooperation; and treaties:
Treaty of Amity and Cooperation)
crises (*see* disputes and crises)

Dalai Lama 12, 14n1 (*see also* China:
Tibet)
decision-making 25
defence 5–9, 11, 14, 18, 20–1, 23, 25,
27n7, 33, 36–8, 41, 45n68, 48–51,
53, 57n34, 57n35 (*see also* Australian
Defence Force (ADF); Australian
Government, Department of Defence;
economics: US defence budget; and
weapons: missiles)
Department of Foreign Affairs and
Trade (*see* Australian Government:
Department of Foreign Affairs and
Trade)
depictions 1, 3–5, 7, 14, 17, 20–2, 25–6,
31–4, 36, 39–42, 47–54
dialogue 4, 17–19, 23, 25–6, 32–3, 44n45,
50
Australia-China Strategic Dialogue
27n7
IISS Shangri-La Dialogue 36
Six-Party Talks 32
Trilateral Security Dialogue 54
diplomacy 2–3, 8, 12, 21–2, 31, 37, 41,
49–50
diplomatic disputes 4, 7, 10, 26–7,
31, 48

diplomatic relations 3, 10, 17–18, 20,
35, 51, 53
disputes and crises 7, 10–14, 17, 22,
24, 32, 41–2, 47–8, 52–3 (*see also*
diplomacy: diplomatic disputes)
Downer, Alexander 1, 7–11, 13–14,
16n37, 17–18, 22–3, 26, 33–5, 38–9,
42, 48–9, 51, 55n5
2004 Beijing statement by 38, 48

East Asia Summit 51
East Timor 54
economics:
Asian Financial Crisis (1997–98) 22
Australia-China Free Trade Agreement
33–4
Australian economy 1, 17, 41, 52–3
China's economic rise 20, 40
Development Import Finance Facility
11, 14
economic growth 19–20, 26–7, 36,
39–40, 53
economic interests 1–2, 4, 8, 17–19,
21, 26, 31, 33–5, 37–8, 40–2, 50
economic opportunity 5, 7–8, 14, 17,
21, 26, 37
economic partnership 1, 6n1, 18,
27n3, 31, 35–6, 41, 50; strategic
economic partnership 1, 17, 26,
27n2, 31, 42
economic prosperity 8, 11, 21, 48
economic relations 2, 4–5, 7–8, 17–
18, 20, 22, 24–6, 28n49, 32–4, 37–8,
42n4, 47–8, 50–3, 55n1
exports 14n2, 28n49, 45n69, 52–3,
56n25
finance scheme 11
imports 28n49
investments 17–18
open market 39
trade domain 42
uranium trade negotiations 12, 14n1
US defence budget 51, 56n21
US-China Economic and Security
Review Commission (2005) 42, 47,
55n1

risk management 23
risk reduction 27n28
Rudd, Kevin 54
    Rudd Government 1, 47
Rumsfeld, Donald 36
Russia 27n7 (*see also* Soviet Union)

Second World War 53
security:
    and stability (of Asia-Pacific region)
      9, 33
    environment 5, 9–10, 14, 18, 23, 47
    global security 25, 33, 54
    influence of 25, 32
    issues 18, 25, 34
    partnership 5, 32, 49, 57n35
    regional security 5, 9–10, 18, 33, 50,
      54–5
    ties/cooperation 5, 9–10, 18, 23, 25,
      32–3, 50, 54–5
Six-Party Talks (*see* dialogue: Six-Party
    Talks)
South China Sea 32
South Korea 9, 31–2, 49 (*see also* Korean
    Peninsula)
Soviet Union 20 (*see also* Russia)
Strahan, Lachlan 2–3, 52–3
strategic:
    alignment 32, 41, 50, 54
    anxiety 2, 4–5, 26, 48, 52–4
    challenge 7–9, 14, 17, 21, 25–6, 32,
      40
    competition 1, 8–9, 20–1, 32, 36, 49
    consideration 25, 32, 41
    development 4, 11, 19–20, 26
    economic partnership 1, 17, 26, 27n3,
     31, 41
    economic relationship 5, 31, 33–4,
     37, 42n4, 48
    engagement 9, 21, 48
    environment 2, 5, 20, 22, 26, 27n7,
     48
    footprint 32, 39
    goal 54
    influence 4, 20, 32, 38, 40, 52
    interaction 2–3, 9

interests 4, 10, 17–19, 21, 26, 31,
    40–1, 50, 52–3
interlocutor 25, 31–2, 34
neighbourhood 53
orientation 1, 4, 13, 35–6, 48
partnership 17–18, 26, 31, 35, 51
perception 2, 5, 20, 54
relationship 1, 5, 31, 34–5, 37, 42, 48,
    51, 53
shockwave 31, 35, 42
stability 8, 11, 21, 25, 48
support 33–4
theory 3
value 31
strategy 4–6, 11, 13–14, 14n1, 22, 25–6,
    34, 47–9, 51, 54, 56n17

Taiwan 1–2, 11–12, 14, 14n1, 17, 22–4,
    26, 32, 34, 36, 38, 44n57, 49, 51
    Democratic Progressive Party in 11
    Taipei 11
    Taiwan-China relations 23
Taiwan Strait:
    March 1996 naval crisis in 1, 9–11,
      13, 14n1, 24, 48, 52
    17 April 2001 naval crisis in 24, 26,
      47, 49
technology 1, 20
    high-tech forces 23–4, 26, 47, 49
territory 20, 24, 49
terrorism 36
    11 September 2001 terrorist attacks
     (*see* United States: 11 September
     2001)
    'war on terror' 2
threat perceptions 1, 20, 24, 32, 41
Tibet (*see* China: Tibet)
trade (*see* economics)
treaties:
    ANZUS Treaty 11, 34 (*see also*
     alliances: ANZUS alliance)
    Comprehensive Test Ban Treaty
     (CTBT) 12, 14
    Treaty of Amity and Cooperation
     (TAC) 51
Trilateral Security Dialogue (*see* dialogue:
    Trilateral Security Dialogue)

www.ingramcontent.com/pod-product-compliance
Lightning Source LLC
Chambersburg PA
CBHW061241270326
41927CB00035B/3468